A HISTORY OF THE WEST VIRGINIA CAPITOL

THE HOUSE OF STATE

JIM WALLACE

Charleston · London

THE History PRESS

Published by The History Press
Charleston, SC 29403
www.historypress.net

Front cover: The West Virginia Capitol's gilded dome is 292 feet high, more than 4 feet higher than the dome of the U.S. Capitol. It is the most prominent feature of the building but also has been the subject of controversy. *Photo by Jim Wallace.*
Back cover, top: A two-ton Czechoslovakian chandelier hangs high in the Capitol's main rotunda, but at times, it has been a threat to the building itself. *Photo by Jim Wallace.*
Back cover, inset: The dome was one of the last parts of the Capitol to be finished in the 1930s.

First published 2012

Manufactured in the United States

ISBN 978.1.60949.691.3

Library of Congress CIP data applied for.

Notice: The information in this book is true and complete to the best of our knowledge. It is offered without guarantee on the part of the author or The History Press. The author and The History Press disclaim all liability in connection with the use of this book.

Contents

ACKNOWLEDGEMENTS

Thanks to: Tom Susman, Rob Ferguson and Oshel Craigo for personal interviews; Tom Susman for photos from Wheeling; Ron Miller for assistance at the Charleston Newspapers Library; John W. Eichleay Jr. and staff at the Heinz History Center for help with the Eichleay Engineers archive photo; various staff members at the Kanawha County Public Library for research assistance; Rachel Coffman for author photo; and Phil Shimer for proofreading.

Chapter 1

From Silver to Gold

The dome of West Virginia's Capitol gleams with gold, but the Capitol is actually the silver lining from a misfortune that befell the state many decades ago.

At the beginning of 1921, the state's Capitol was an eighty-five-room Victorian building with towers, dormers and a mansard roof. It stood in downtown Charleston. On January 3, 1921, a great fire destroyed it.

For the people of Charleston, as well as residents of the state in general, it was a big loss, but it set the stage for a big gain. Had the Capitol not burned down, it is anyone's guess how long that building would have continued to serve as the seat of state government, but there is little doubt that it would not have remained adequate for the state's needs for much longer into the twentieth century. In 1887, the Victorian Capitol was big enough to hold all of the offices of state agencies, but by 1903, state government supplemented it with an annex built across the street. However, in its downtown location, room for more expansion around the Capitol was limited.

Another strike against the Victorian-era Capitol was that it just did not look like what most people expect a capitol to look like. Although it was grand for its time, it looked more like a big schoolhouse. Its continued use would have made it more difficult for West Virginia to portray itself as a modern state.

West Virginians were fortunate that, within weeks of the fire, the legislature created a commission to plan for construction of a replacement that would be grander and better suited to the needs of the future. Part of the state's good fortune was that planning and construction of the new Capitol began in

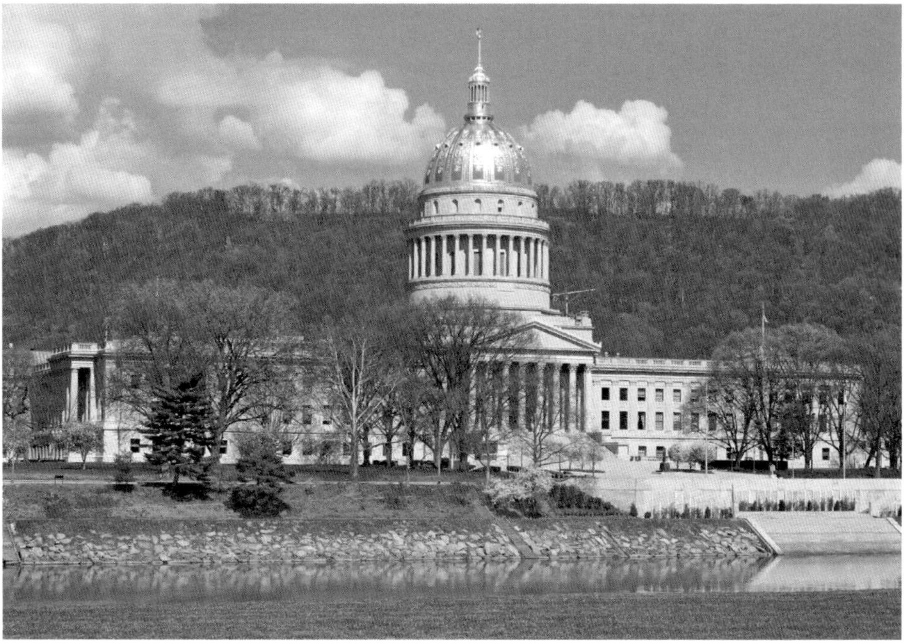

West Virginia's Capitol now sits along the Kanawha River on Charleston's East End, but the seat of state government has not always been located there. *Photo by Jim Wallace.*

the 1920s, when the nation's economy was booming. By the time the Capitol was finished and dedicated in 1932, the United States was in the depths of the Great Depression. Perhaps if the old Capitol had burned down a decade later than it did, West Virginia might not have been as willing to spend almost $9.5 million on the new Capitol. The state could have ended up with a structure that was much less grand and subsequently much less enduring.

Stan Cohen and Richard Andre also shared this view in their 1989 book, *Capitols of West Virginia: A Pictorial History*, when they wrote that if work to replace the old Capitol had been delayed ten years or more, the result would have been a more modest, modern building. "In a certain way it can be said that the then tragic fire was indeed providential, as it enabled the state to construct a truly magnificent Capitol that would have been economically impossible in the 1930s and not feasible during the wartime 1940s," they wrote.

Thus, although the destruction of the Victorian Capitol in 1921 seemed like a great loss to the state at the time, out of the dark clouds of smoke from that fire arose what truly was a silver lining: a Capitol that could be a point of pride for West Virginians well into the future.

Chapter 2

Moving Capital

West Virginia was the only state to be formed directly as a result of the Civil War. It is perhaps not surprising then that a state born from such turmoil remained unsettled for many years on where its capital should be. Once again, it was a North-South conflict, a less bloody but still hard-fought civil war that took five times as long as the nation's Civil War to end.

The seeds of West Virginia's separation as a state were sown well before Virginia seceded from the Union, but secession exacerbated the discontent among residents to the west of the Alleghenies, particularly those in the northwestern part of Virginia. They long had coped with different geography and economic patterns than eastern Virginians. The westerners and easterners also disagreed over spending money on public improvements and political representation in Richmond, as well as the issue of slavery.

Just as the nation's founding fathers met in the Continental Congress in Philadelphia while they considered independence from Britain, Virginians opposed to the state's secession from the Union met in Wheeling in two conventions beginning in 1861. Although some wanted to move directly to the formation of a new state, others objected, partly because such an action seemed to be unconstitutional. At the Second Wheeling Convention, the representatives decided instead to first form the Reorganized (or Restored) Government of Virginia, which purported to be Virginia's true government but was just a steppingstone toward the formation of a new state. Francis Pierpont became governor of the reorganized state on June 20, 1861.

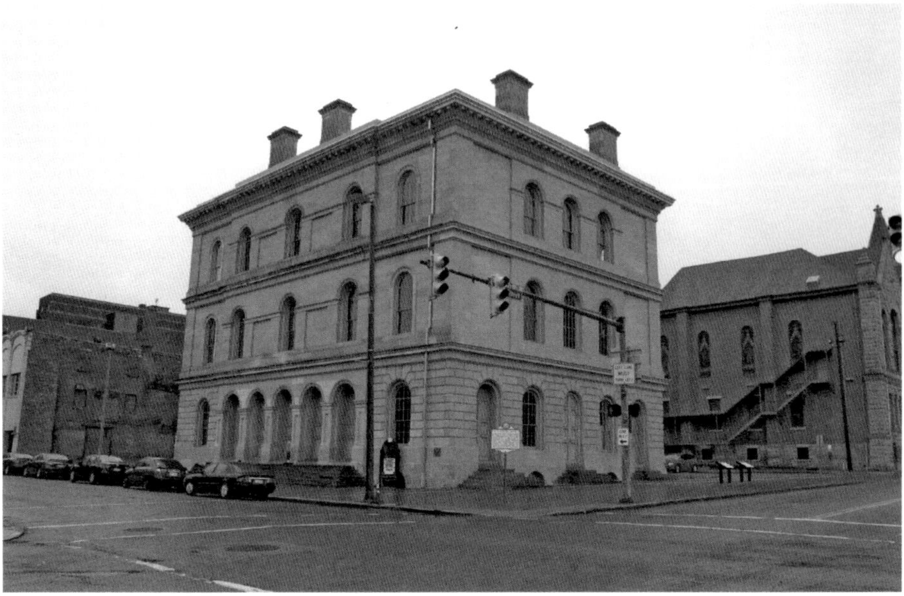

Independence Hall in Wheeling never served as a capitol for West Virginia, but it was for the so-called Reorganized State of Virginia. It also was the place where the steps toward statehood began. *Photo by Tom Susman.*

The meeting place for those leaders was the U.S. Custom House, which had opened in 1859. For two years, it served as the capitol of the Reorganized State of Virginia. Because of the role it played in those years, the building later became known as West Virginia Independence Hall, and beginning in 1979, it became a state museum.

However, the restored Virginia government was only a means to an end. It has been described as a "state of convenience," which allowed the western Virginians to get around a constitutional provision that could have prevented West Virginia's split from Virginia. Under the U.S. Constitution, carving a state out of an existing state can occur only if the original state grants its permission. In the case of West Virginia, residents did not request permission from the Virginia government based in Richmond that was part of the Confederacy; the so-called Reorganized State of Virginia based in Wheeling essentially gave that permission to itself. Representatives at the Second Wheeling Convention decided to pursue that course in August 1861.

The proposed creation of the new state went to a referendum on October 24, 1861. Based on the 1860 census, about sixty-nine thousand voters would have been eligible to participate, but only about 28 percent of them did.

Only the northern tier of western Virginia provided overwhelming support for the new state. "The farther south you got, the less interested the voters were in forming a new state and staying with the Union," Dr. Billy Joe Peyton, associate professor of history at West Virginia State University, said in a 2012 lecture. From the Kanawha River south, people had virtually no interest in separation from Virginia, but their counties were incorporated into the new state anyhow. That regional split would influence West Virginia politics for decades to come.

President Lincoln's cabinet was divided over whether to accept the new state, but Lincoln signed a bill on December 31, 1862, to authorize West Virginia's admission as a state. He followed up on April 20, 1863, with a proclamation that statehood would become effective on June 20, 1863.

A CAPITAL ISSUE

In his first message to West Virginia's first legislature, Governor Arthur Boreman said, "I recommend that you take speedy action for the establishment of a permanent seat of government. I know it is said by some that it would be best to wait until the war is ended, but I fear if the question is not settled by the present legislature, it will, in a short time, enter into contests for office throughout the state, and thus become a matter of contention for years to come." Legislators did not heed his recommendation, and his fear was realized.

The seat of government for the new state remained in Wheeling but not at the Custom House. Instead, the state borrowed a three-story structure with a combination of Greek Revival and Italianate architectural styles to serve as West Virginia's first Capitol. It had been built in 1858 at the corner of Fifteenth and Eoff Streets to serve as the second home of Linsly Institute. Wheeling lawyer Noah Linsly founded the institute in 1814 as the first preparatory school west of the Allegheny Mountains.

The Linsly building might have been adequate for state government in those early years, but it did not take long for some political leaders to consider a move, not just to another building, but to Charleston. That was despite Wheeling's attributes as a capital. As Peyton said, "Wheeling was the only true city that we had." He called Wheeling "the hub of industry in western Virginia," while Charleston was described as "a lovely village" in 1870. Charleston did not yet have a railroad, and it had made only a limited number of improvements on its riverfront. A few turnpikes came through

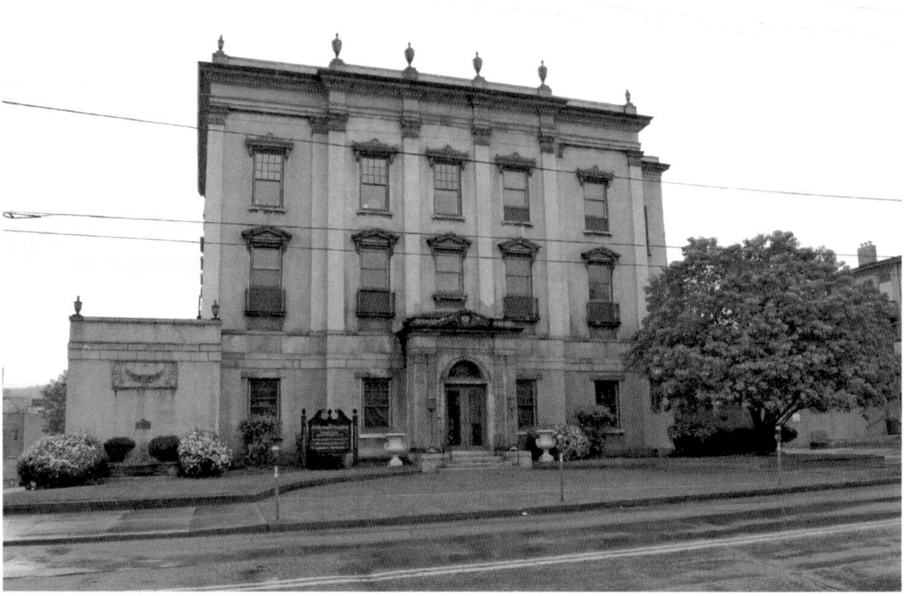

The Linsly Institute building in Wheeling was just a few years old when state officials obtained its use for West Virginia's first Capitol. *Photo by Tom Susman.*

Charleston, but turnpike travel was rough, slow and sometimes dangerous. By contrast, Wheeling had the B&O Railroad, the uppermost four-season navigation on the Ohio River and the National Road. "If you looked at the two places, Charleston would not be your pick for a capital, except for the political events that were about to transpire," Peyton said.

Those "political events" involved the settling of differences in West Virginia that had lingered from the Civil War. During the postwar period, former Confederates were limited in their ability to participate in political affairs in most southern states until Reconstruction came to an end in 1877. But in West Virginia, restrictions began to ease on them soon after the war ended. "By 1868, our state Legislature becomes more conservative," Peyton said, and in those days, Democrats were the conservatives. By 1870, Democrats swept the elections in West Virginia. Thus, the state swung from Republican control when it was created in 1863 to Democratic control in less than a decade. Democratic control meant that more southern West Virginians were in power, and they tended to favor moving the capital south.

Charleston bolstered support for the move when, in January 1869, the people of the city decided to offer $50,000 for the construction of a new building, a Capitol state officials would not have to share with a school. Within a month, the House of Delegates voted 29–23 and the Senate voted 17–4 to make Charleston the capital beginning April 1, 1870.

GOING SOUTH

On March 28, 1870, Governor William Stevenson and other state officials boarded *Mountain Boy*, a steamboat loaded with the state's official papers and other items. It did not take much persuasion—or any money—to get the *Mountain Boy*'s captain, James Newton, to take the job. "I will come with cannon, music and floating flags and will consider the honor sufficient pay," he said in accepting the duty. He operated a packet service on the Ohio and Kanawha Rivers, so Newton was already familiar with the route. The government leaders traveled down the Ohio River with a stop at Stevenson's hometown of Parkersburg and then up the Kanawha River to Charleston. A local delegation and an artillery salute greeted them at midday on March 30.

However, the government arrived several months before the new Capitol was ready. State leaders again had to borrow space, this time in bank buildings. The governor, secretary of state, state school superintendent, adjutant general and attorney general did business in the old Bank of the West, while the auditor worked out of the rear of the new Bank of the West and the treasurer worked out of the rear of Merchants' Bank. The state library was housed at St. John's Protestant Episcopal Church.

Construction of the new, three-story Capitol, built with hand-cut stone, was finished that December. Architects in Cincinnati chose an Italianate style with Romanesque touches. Dr. John P. Hale, a prominent Charleston physician and businessman, led the corporation that built the Capitol, and he ended up bearing much of its cost of about $80,000. But he also built the Hale House Hotel just blocks from the Capitol at the corner of Hale Street and Kanawha Street (later Boulevard). Therefore, he benefited from having legislators and others come to Charleston to do business at the Capitol.

State officials moved into the new Capitol on December 20, 1870. It was located near the present-day intersection of Lee Street and Capitol Street, which is the reason that Charleston has a Capitol Street almost two miles away from the current Capitol. A historical marker on the Lee Street Triangle commemorates the original Capitol location.

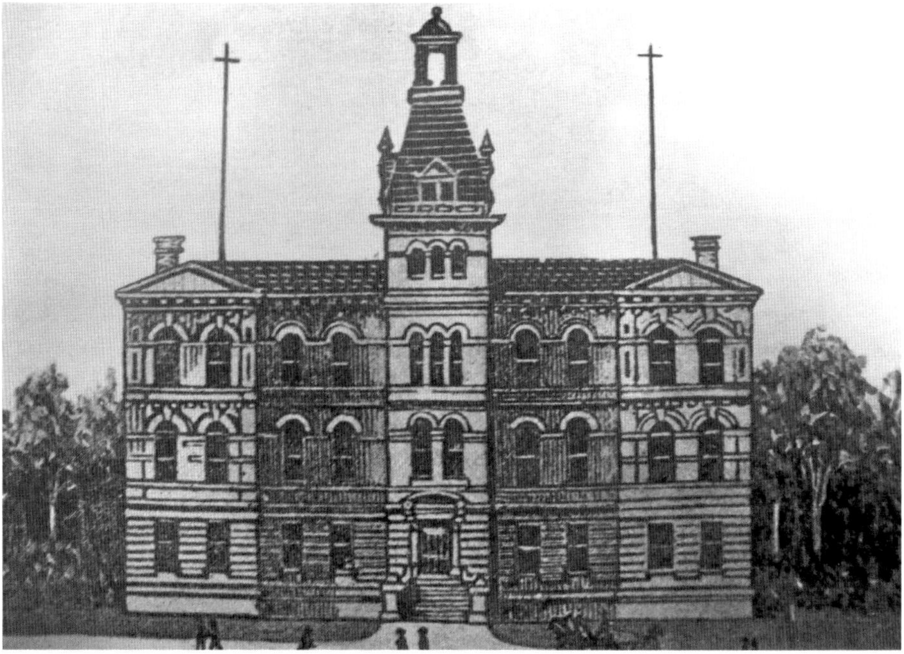

West Virginia's second Capitol, as depicted in this drawing, was the first one built in Charleston and the first created specifically to serve as a seat of government. *Photo courtesy of Charleston Newspapers.*

Governor Stevenson said of the new Capitol, "It is, as you cannot fail to observe, a neat, commodious and substantial structure and reflects much credit upon the public spirited citizens under whose management it was completed and finished."

WHEELING STRIKES BACK

But the citizens of Wheeling were not content to let go of the distinction of being the state capital even after the government had gone to Charleston. From their perspective, Wheeling was more appropriate for the seat of government, not only because it was the birthplace of the state but also because it was a more substantial community that was growing rapidly. Wheeling already had 19,280 residents in the 1870 census and grew to 30,737 by 1880. In 1870, Charleston had only 3,162 residents and grew to only 4,192 by 1880.

The people of Wheeling soon decided what worked for Charleston could work for them. They offered to build an even grander Capitol and approved a $100,000 bond issue to do it. They also argued that, even with the Hale House Hotel, Charleston did not have enough accommodations for legislators and others who did business with the state. On February 20, 1875, the legislature voted to accept Wheeling's offer.

"Essentially, the Legislature caved to complaints about Charleston being too hard to get to," Peyton said. "Indeed, if you weren't located along the Kanawha or one of its tributaries, it would be difficult."

However, the move back to Wheeling was not as simple as the move away from it. First, Governor John Jeremiah Jacob, a Democrat, expressed his displeasure by letting the bill to move the capital become law without his signature. (However, Jacob later seemed to warm up to Wheeling. He remained a resident of Wheeling after his second term as governor ended in 1877, despite his initial reluctance to move there.) Then on March 30, several Charleston citizens—led by John Slack and John Cotton—got a court injunction to prevent state records and other property from making the move. Judge Evermont Ward, who granted the injunction, set a hearing date for May 21. Another judge, Joseph Smith, dissolved that injunction on May 18. The plaintiffs appealed to the state Supreme Court, which recognized the appeal on May 20 but took until September 13 to rule in favor of the move to Wheeling.

Thus, when state officials boarded the steamboat *Emma Graham* in Charleston on May 21, they were on their own as they headed down the Kanawha. At Point Pleasant, they transferred to a different steamboat, the *Chesapeake*, for the trip up the Ohio, but when they arrived in Wheeling on May 23, they still had no idea when they might be reunited with the state's records and other property.

Although it had taken only one steamer to bring the records to Charleston in 1870, that was not enough in 1875. By then, state government had grown so much that it required the steamer *Iron Valley* and two barges to transport the records and other property back to the Northern Panhandle. The vessels left Charleston on September 22.

Yet once again, government officials were in a capital without a Capitol. It took until December 4, 1876, for the new building to be ready for their use. While they waited on construction, state officials used the Linsly Institute building again as a temporary capitol, and the legislature met nearby at Washington Hall until a fire ruined it on November 30, 1875. The new Capitol was built of stone in a combination of Greek Revival and

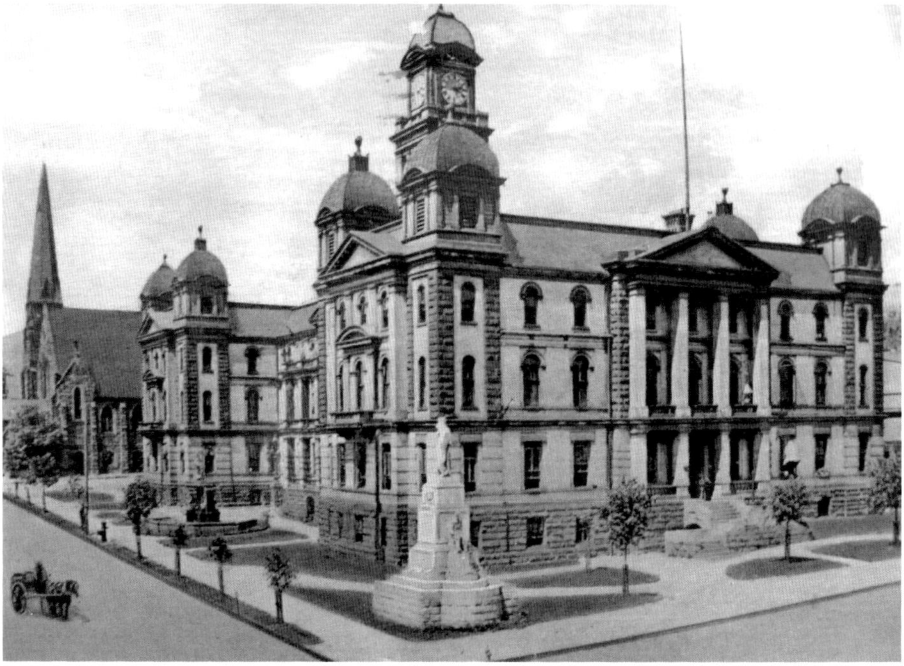

West Virginia's third Capitol was the second one in Wheeling. It later served as a city hall, as shown in this early twentieth-century postcard, and county courthouse until it was torn down in 1956 and replaced with a more modern building.

Romanesque architecture. It was four stories tall, had two large wings and was topped by a cupola.

"So in addition to actually moving state government, each of the capitals is trying to outdo each other in building new and improved facilities," Peyton said. "The Capitol is getting more ornate and larger with every move."

CITIES CRAVE CAPITAL

However, the nice, new Capitol failed to settle the battle between Wheeling and Charleston. Wheeling's location halfway up the skinny Northern Panhandle made more sense as a capital during the Civil War because it was solidly within Union territory and far from the reaches of Confederate forces. By contrast, Charleston was divided between northern and southern loyalists and was occupied by Confederate forces for about six weeks in

1862 before the Union retook it and held onto it. But as West Virginia grew into statehood, Wheeling's location became more inconvenient. As the *Huntington Advertiser* put it on October 28, 1875, Wheeling was located "in a remote corner of the State, far more convenient to the States of Ohio and Pennsylvania than it is to West Virginia."

Charleston had the advantage of being more centrally located than Wheeling, although it was still quite a distance from the exact center of the state. Charleston also began to catch up with Wheeling in terms of connections to the rest of the nation. The first railroad, the Chesapeake and Ohio Railway, arrived in Charleston on the south side of the Kanawha in 1873, but it took until 1884 for the north side of the river to be connected by the Kanawha and Ohio (later Kanawha and Michigan) Railroad.

Yet even while Wheeling and Charleston battled over the right to be the capital, some West Virginians thought neither was the best choice. On June 5, 1875, the *Clarksburg Telegram* wrote: "Neither Charleston or Wheeling can retain the capital for many years, as both are too inconvenient of access from all sections of the State. Sooner or later it must be placed in a more central location, as are other State capitals, corner lots and speculators to the contrary notwithstanding."

Legislators had barely settled into the second Capitol in Wheeling when they decided in 1877 to put the permanent location of the capital up to a vote of the people in an election scheduled for August 7, 1877. And apparently because southern Democrats were in control, they declined to include Wheeling among the choices. In addition to Charleston, the alternatives for voters included Clarksburg, which was about as close to the geographical center of the state as Charleston. But the strange third alternative was Martinsburg, far in the Eastern Panhandle, which would have been a more inconvenient location than Wheeling for most West Virginians. The reasons for the inclusion of Martinsburg are unclear, but one effect it likely had was to siphon off votes from some Eastern Panhandle residents who might otherwise have been likely to favor the northern alternative of Clarksburg rather than Charleston. Peyton said that might be a good explanation for the inclusion of Martinsburg, because "aside from its significance to the B&O Railroad as a major rail center, that would be the only reason for it to be included."

A few prominent figures campaigned actively for Charleston. Two of them were John E. Kenna, a congressman from Charleston who later served in the U.S. Senate, and Romeo H. Freer, who went on to become attorney general of West Virginia and then a judge. They arranged to travel with a circus, which gave them a few minutes during each show to make their pitch for Charleston.

Another was African American educator Booker T. Washington, who grew up in Malden, about five miles from Charleston. "At the close of my school year in Washington I was very pleasantly surprised to receive, from a committee of white people in Charleston, an invitation to canvass the state in the interests of that city," he wrote in his 1901 book, *Up from Slavery*. "This invitation I accepted, and spent nearly three months in speaking in various parts of the state. Charleston was successful in winning the prize, and is now the permanent seat of government."

The election results were 41,243 votes for Charleston, 29,942 for Clarksburg and 8,046 for Martinsburg.

THE FINAL CAPITAL MOVE

Unlike with the previous two moves, state officials took their time returning to Charleston. Wheeling remained the capital until 1885. When state government moved back to Charleston, it required two steamboats and a barge. One steamboat, the *Chesapeake*, carried state officials. The other, the *Belle Prince*, towed the barge, named *Nick Crawley*, laden with state records and other property. Although Charleston officially became the capital again on May 1, 1885, the boats arrived on May 3.

State leaders eventually moved into a three-story, Victorian-style Capitol, built at a cost of $389,923, in the same downtown location as the earlier Capitol. The new building was said to have incorporated parts of the old building. The building had a 194-foot-high clock tower, eighty-five rooms and a slate roof. The front was 230 feet wide. The central hall was 180 feet long from front to back, and two parallel wings were 130 feet long. The Capitol occupied an entire block between Capitol and Dickinson Streets and between Washington Street and Lee Street.

Although Charleston had several years to prepare to resume its role as capital, the new Capitol was not ready when the government returned. It took until 1887 before officials had full use of the building.

Meanwhile, the building left behind in Wheeling remained a seat of government—but local, not state—for seven more decades. Eventually, its clock tower and cupolas were removed, and in 1956, the entire building was torn down. A square-cut, rectangular building of less architectural

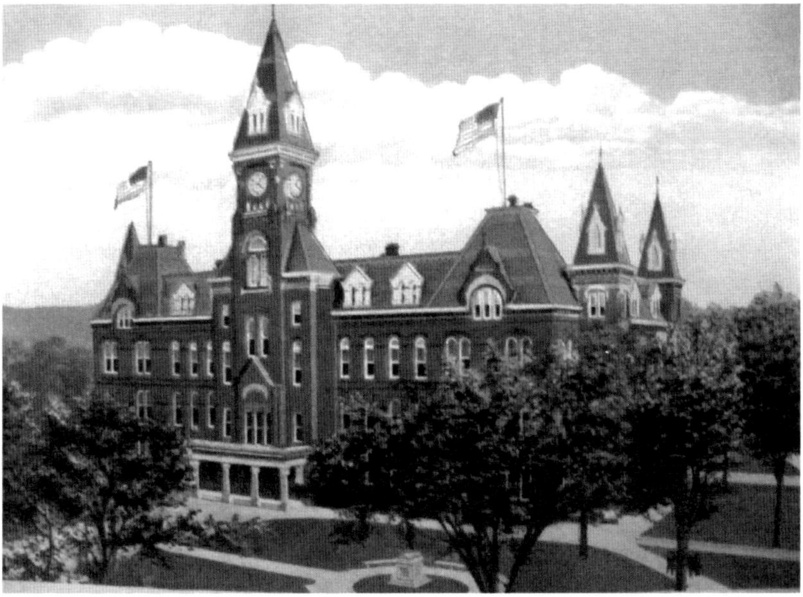

West Virginia's fourth Capitol, as seen in this early twentieth-century postcard, occupied the same block in downtown Charleston as the second Capitol.

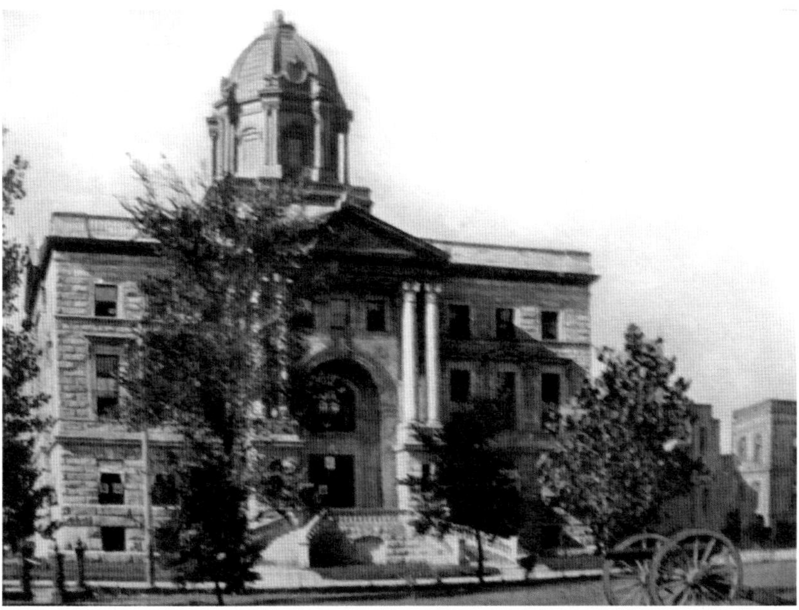

The Capitol Annex, seen in this postcard view, gave state government more office space beginning in 1903. After the new Capitol was built in Charleston's East End, the Capitol Annex served as Charleston's public library for many years.

distinction replaced it as the City-County Building. Despite that, the building that served as Wheeling's second Capitol actually survived thirty-five years longer than the building in Charleston that replaced it.

It took less than two decades for state government to outgrow the new Capitol in Charleston. In 1899, state officials made plans to build the Capitol Annex across Lee Street from the Capitol between Hale and Dickinson Streets. It was designed to house the Supreme Court, offices for the auditor and treasurer, the state library, the law library and state archives. Construction on the annex, a stone building with a dome, was completed in 1903 at a cost of about $250,000.

Chapter 3

Decision Born from Fire

It was fortunate for the state that some offices, including the state archives, had moved into the Capitol Annex. Not so fortunate was the decision by someone that the Capitol's attic was a good place to store guns and about fifty thousand rounds of ammunition, including some that had been confiscated in 1919 from people involved in the mine wars, which raged on and off throughout the southern coalfields for a decade beginning in 1912.

At about 3:15 p.m. on January 3, 1921, smoke began rising from the southern end of the top of the Capitol, apparently from the attic above the Senate chamber. Within minutes, flames leaped out of the roof, and thousands of people gathered to watch the great fire.

"Smoke was first noticed coming out of the windows of the top floor of the building by persons passing along the streets and, before any of the state house attaches were aware that the building was on fire, the alarm had been turned in to headquarters and the [fire] department was on the way," the *Charleston Gazette* reported. "The flames spread rapidly through the top story of the building and soon communicated to the north side over the house of delegates' hall, and it was soon evident that it was but a matter of time until the entire building was doomed."

Governor John Cornwell, who had been working in his office, was reported to be one of the last officials to leave the building. He went to the Governor's Mansion across the street to watch the destruction of the Capitol.

"Of course, this fire is little short of a calamity to the state because of the records that have been destroyed in the various departments which

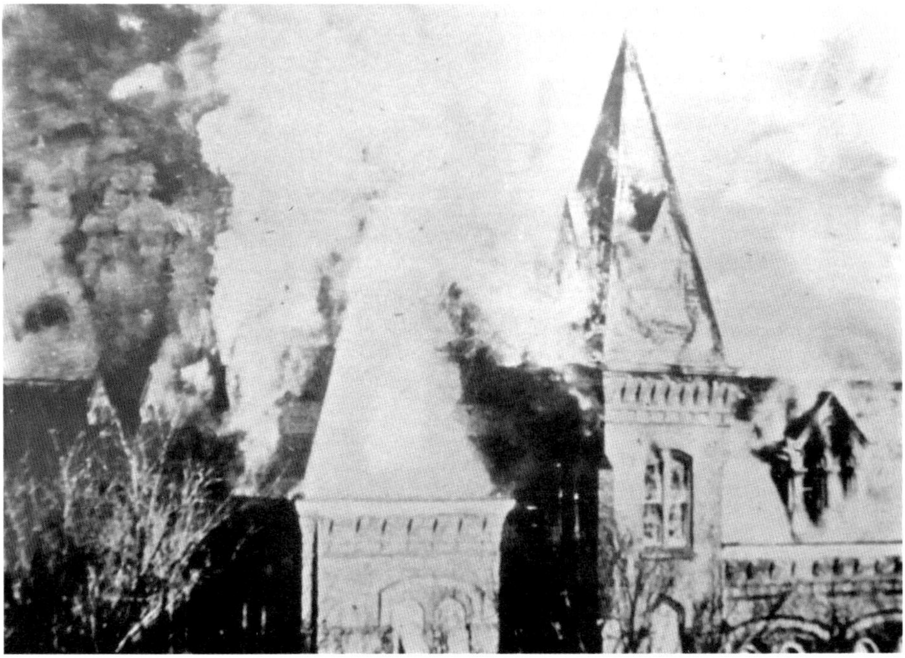

Above: The fire that broke out in the attic of the Capitol on January 3, 1921, soon spread and destroyed the building. *Photo courtesy of Charleston Newspapers.*

Opposite top: The Charleston Fire Department used the Kanawha Pumper in the futile effort to extinguish the fire that destroyed the Capitol. The pumper is now displayed at the Charleston Civic Center. *Photo by Jim Wallace.*

Opposite bottom: The Capitol burned from late afternoon into the evening of January 3, 1921. *Photo courtesy of Charleston Newspapers.*

will occasion inconvenience to many people," Cornwell said. He expressed less concern about monetary loss, because the state had all of its buildings insured for about $6 million.

The city's entire fire department, which still used some horse-drawn engines, battled the fire but was little match for it. "Inaccessible to the firemen, it was soon evident that the building was doomed," the *Gazette* wrote. "The fire would have defied the best departments and equipments in any city and from the start the efforts of the city fire fighters to compete with the flames were futile." One volunteer fireman, Charles Walker, died when a wall collapsed on him.

The ammunition in the attic made the fire more spectacular with fireworks and explosions, which caused many of the spectators to pull back from the

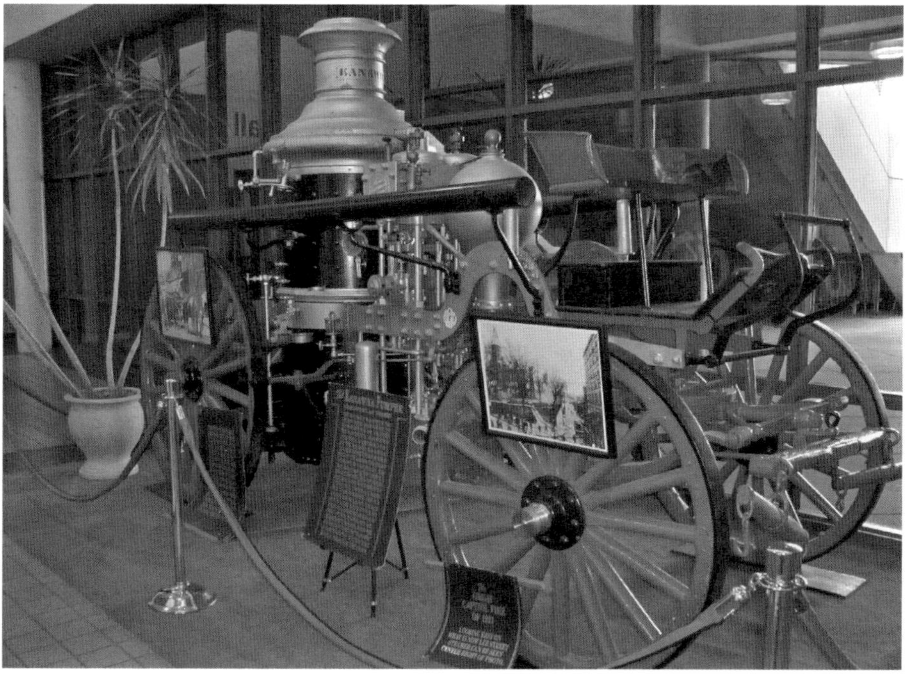

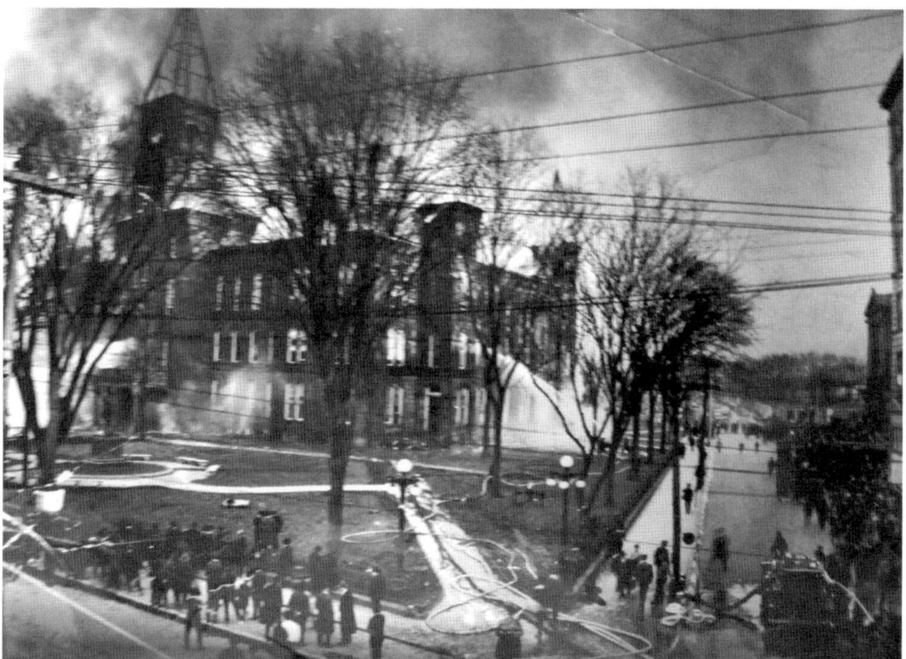

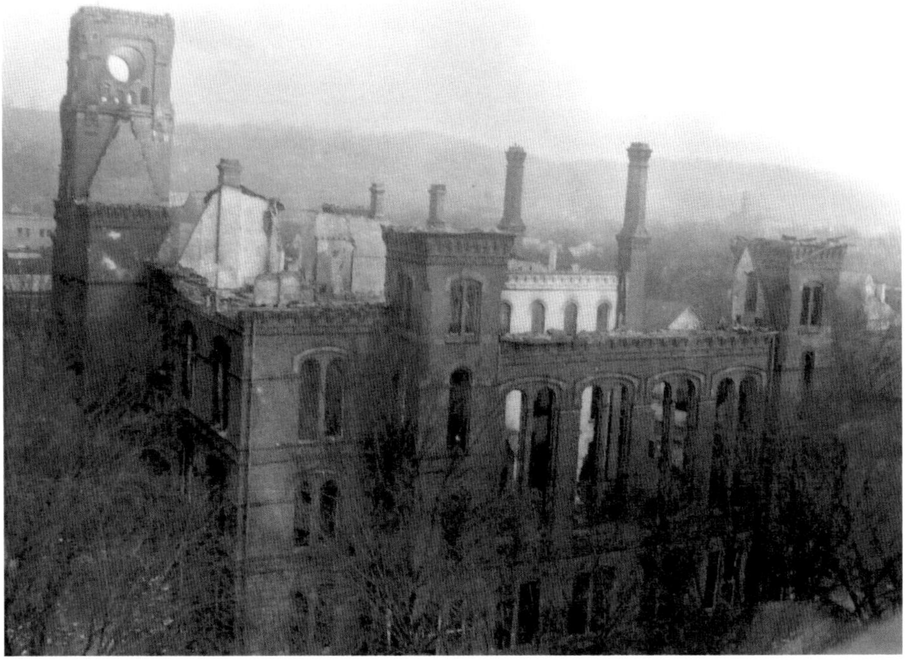

The walls of the Capitol stood as an empty shell after the fire. *Photo courtesy of Charleston Newspapers.*

building. As E.V. King of the West Virginia Inspection Bureau put it in his report, filed on January 20, 1921, "The exploding small arms ammunition caused considerable excitement among the spectators but no one was injured from flying shells." It was reported that people picked up many expended shells from the Capitol's lawn after the fire.

The *Gazette* reported, "From 3 o'clock in the afternoon until dark the flames ate their way from the lofts to the cellars, from wing to wing, until as dusk settled over the scene, the havoc had been so complete that the once-beautiful state house was completely destroyed, leaving only charred walls and blackened remnants of the seat of government."

King, in his inspection report, concluded: "Owing to the highly inflammable nature of the building, the progress of the fire before the alarm was received and the absence of division walls to roof, it is questionable whether the building could have been saved from total destruction, but it is possible that the fire might have been confined to the Senate wing had all the available hose lines been immediately connected to pumping engines and concentrated on the narrow section connecting the Senate wing with the rest of the building." He decided that a lesson of the fire was that automatic sprinkler systems were necessary in public buildings of ordinary joist construction.

Some people suspected that arson had caused the destruction of the Capitol. Charleston police and the state fire marshal's office questioned Arnold Gladwell, a thirty-year-old drug addict, after he was rumored to have been involved, but he denied any connection with the fire. Others suggested that someone might have wanted to destroy records stored at the Capitol. Years later, J.K. Gies, the Capitol's head custodian at the time of the fire, reportedly told a granddaughter that he had discovered, just days before the fire, a few men in the attic playing dice by candlelight and chased them out. The use of candlelight near the ammunition in the attic could have caused the fire either accidentally or on purpose, but no one ever knew for sure what happened. The fire department attributed the fire to faulty electric wiring, but Capitol maintenance workers claimed the wiring was in good condition.

FIRE REKINDLES CAPITAL COMPETITION

Out of the fire sprang opportunity. It was a commercial opportunity for the Walker Dry Goods Company of 112–114 Capitol Street. On the day after the fire, the store ran an advertisement in the *Gazette* with the headline: "STATEHOUSE BURNED! PRICES SLASHED AT WALKER'S."

Under that, it said, "These are the two big headlines in today's news—The former a disaster—the latter your opportunity to save." The ad offered women's apparel at discounts of 25 percent to 50 percent off, similar savings on home furnishings, children's apparel at 20 percent to 25 percent off and toys at half price. Perhaps it was an already-planned after-Christmas sale that suddenly became a fire sale.

Just as suddenly, the fire also reignited contention over whether Charleston or another city should be the capital. The *Gazette* reported: "Governor John J. Cornwell received a wire from Wheeling last night asking that the regular session of the state legislature be held in that city, but on account of having made practically positive arrangements for the session to be held here, did not accept that offer."

However, the civic leaders of Charleston did not need to wait to read the newspaper to realize the threat to their city. That same edition of the *Gazette* contained an ad for a special meeting called by the chamber of commerce for 10:30 on the morning after the fire at the Hotel Kanawha. The next day, the paper reported that chamber members agreed unanimously to find shelter for "homeless state departments with a minimum of delay."

That was accomplished. The governor, secretary of state, adjutant general, pardon attorney and Department of Public Safety worked out of the state armory on Capitol Street. Other officials went to various other facilities, including the Red Cross Tea Room, the Elks Club, the Masonic Temple, the Davidson Building, the Morrison Building, the Methodist Episcopal Church and the Scottish Rite Cathedral. The Senate held its session in the YMCA auditorium, while the House of Delegates used the Baptist Temple.

But more importantly, as the *Gazette* reported, the chamber decided "to strike quickly and effectively for a new state house that will more adequately express the importance of West Virginia." Members wanted the city to purchase all the property in the downtown block bounded by Washington, Broad (now Leon Sullivan Way), Lee and Dickinson Streets and offer it to the state as a site for a new Capitol.

"They are already having the property in view appraised and are otherwise proceeding in dead earnest to make what is proposed a reality and to get the 'jump' on any other city which might see an opportunity to get the capitol away from us," the *Gazette* reported.

The businessmen of Charleston were right to be worried, because other cities began readying their bids to become the new capital as soon as they heard about the fire. This time, Clarksburg was the main challenger. An Associated Press report on January 4, the day after the fire, said that the Kiwanis Club in Clarksburg had "adopted a resolution calling for concerted action among Clarksburgers in an endeavor to have the state house located in the city. A committee was appointed and this committee at once began planning for a campaign to interest local capital in subscribing to a fund to purchase a suitable site for the building in the event the legislature could be induced to move it."

But Clarksburg was not the only city in the running. "The rumor persists that Wheeling, Parkersburg and Clarksburg are working to knock out Charleston first and then decide on one or the other of those cities for the capitol," the *Gazette* reported on January 16, 1921. "This may not be the deliberate plan agreed upon, but that is frankly stated, around the hotel lobbies, as the combined purpose, by boosters for some, if not all, of those cities."

An article in the *Clarksburg Exponent* confirmed that at least two of those cities were working together:

> *Owing to the geographical location of Charleston which completely isolates a large portion of the counties of the northern and eastern part of the state a concerted effort will be made to remove the capitol from its present location to a city further to the north with preference being given to Clarksburg and Parkersburg, both of whom have entered actively into the race for the coveted position.*
>
> *Telegrams and letters poured into the city yesterday in large numbers from some of the most prominent men and legislators in the counties to the north, east, west and several from the south admonishing Clarksburg to awake to the realization that this is the golden opportunity to wrest from Charleston the state capitol and bring it to the central part of the state where a greater number of the state solons could reach the capitol with the least inconvenience possible.*

The *Exponent* article also included the contents of telegrams exchanged by the presidents of the chambers of commerce in Parkersburg and Clarksburg pledging support to each other over Charleston in the competition to be the capital.

Clarksburg's Citizens' Capital Committee published a pamphlet titled "Fifty Reasons Why State Capital Should Be Located at Clarksburg, W.Va." Among the reasons offered were that the community was the geographical center of forty of the fifty-five counties and that it was accessible 365 days a year by railroad, electric lines and state highways.

QUICK DECISIONS ON NEW CAPITOLS

In the midst of such lobbying efforts, West Virginia's leaders wasted little time before they began considering at least a temporary replacement for the Capitol. By January 14, they decided to put up a building a block away from the destroyed Capitol at the northwest corner of Washington and Capitol Streets, where the Daniel Boone Hotel (now the office building known as 405 Capitol Street) later would be built. It was built fast—in just forty-two days—and cheaply, out of wood and a type of wallboard called "beaver board," for about $225,000. For good reason, that building received the nickname the "Pasteboard Capitol." It suffered the same fate as its predecessor when a fire broke out about 2:30 p.m. on March 2, 1927, and consumed

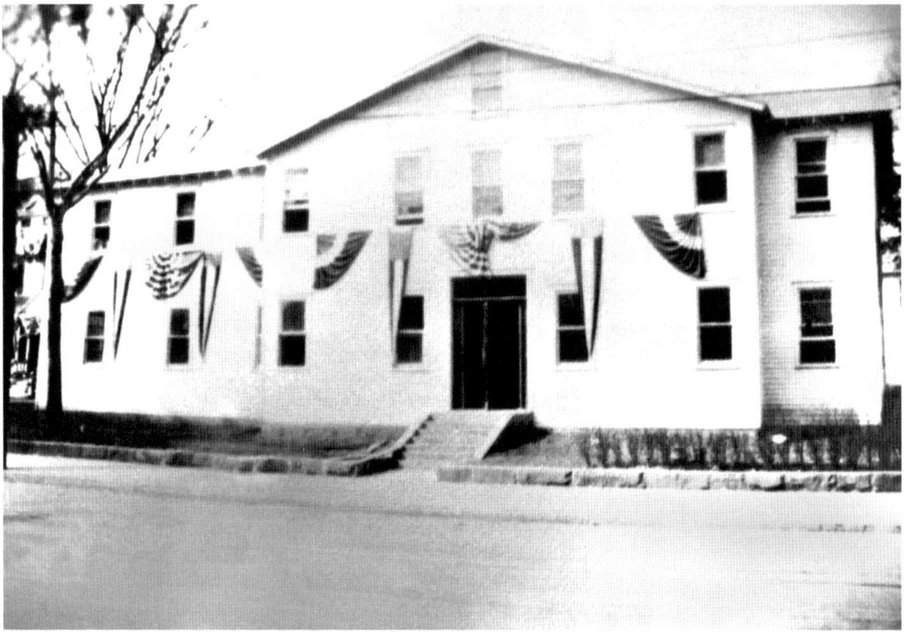

The "Pasteboard Capitol" housed government offices from 1921 until it also burned down in 1927. *Photo courtesy of Kanawha County Public Library (1137).*

the building within half an hour. Although the fire was believed to have started on the second floor or on the roof, the *Gazette* reported that "many occupants of the second floor said it appeared in offices so quickly it seemed to have started everywhere at once." The nine offices that had been housed in the "Pasteboard Capitol" had to be relocated to other temporary homes. Fortunately, some state offices already had moved into the first unit that had been built for the new Capitol in the East End of the city.

The legislature began laying plans for a new, permanent Capitol shortly after construction of the "Pasteboard Capitol" had begun. Lawmakers soon dampened the hopes of some and fears of others that a city other than Charleston would become the capital. On January 21, 1921, the Senate voted 20–10 to approve a resolution in favor of building a new Capitol in Charleston. The senators defeated amendments offered by Senator Harvey Harmer of Clarksburg. Harmer charged that Charleston supporters, which the *Exponent* called "the Kanawha County Hog Combine," had made attempts to "corrupt, browbeat and coerce the members of this legislature."

Legislators also adopted a resolution to form a commission to figure out how big a new Capitol should be and how to build it. Soon, Governor

Ephraim Morgan, who took office in March 1921, received authority to appoint the Capitol Building Commission. The commission initially consisted of Morgan, Senate President Gohen Arnold, House Speaker Edwin Keatley, Secretary of State Houston Young and a few unelected citizens: William McKell, Herbert Fitzpatrick, Fred Staunton and Price Whitaker. The composition of the commission changed several times over more than a decade. One significant change occurred when Young, who had served as the commission's secretary, resigned from it in September 1923 to allow Charleston resident Bonner Hill to become a full-time, paid secretary. That was a notable change, because Hill had overseen the construction of Charleston City Hall and brought that experience to the process.

AN ARCHITECT AND A LOCATION

Among the first big decisions the commission had to make was the selection of an architect. On July 21, 1921, members chose Cass Gilbert of New York City. He was responsible for designing quite a number of outstanding buildings, including the Woolworth Building in New York, which was then the tallest building in the world. Gilbert also had designed government buildings, including the capitols of Minnesota and Arkansas, the U.S. Treasury Annex and the main libraries in St. Louis, New Haven and Detroit. Later, he was the architect for the U.S. Supreme Court Building.

As the 1974 application to include the Capitol in the National Register of Historic Places put it, "Gilbert's selection as architect came only after the Building Commission considered the leaders in the profession. It found that Mr. Gilbert had more to his credit and that he came more highly recommended than any other member of his profession."

Choosing the architect was easier than choosing the site for the new Capitol. As many as seventeen sites were proposed. A drawing in the State Archives shows what the Capitol might have looked like sitting on the hill overlooking downtown Charleston. One map proposed a location on "Hill-crest Mountain" (better known today as the Hillcrest Drive area of Charleston), which would have had the Capitol on the hill above its current location. At least two maps and other documents supported building the new Capitol downtown along Capitol Street, where the

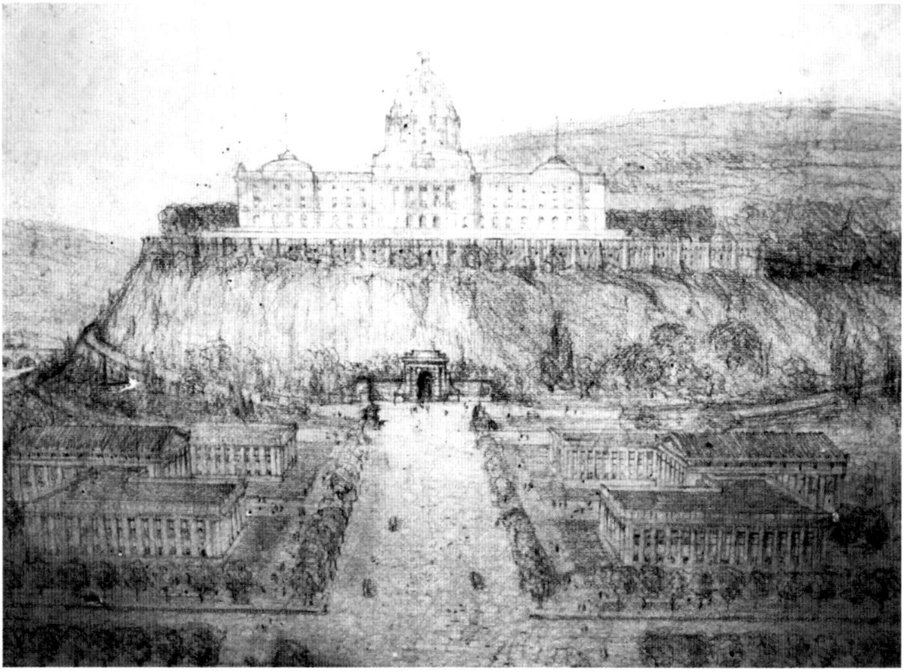

One proposal for the new Capitol was to put it on the hill overlooking downtown Charleston, as shown in this 1920s sketch.

previous capitol had been located. Many citizens in Charleston favored that site because of its proximity to the business district. J.S. Darst, the state auditor, suggested adding eight to ten floors onto the Capitol Annex for a skyscraper Capitol. "The building is one of the best constructed in the state and is practically fireproof," he said. But Governor Morgan expressed preference for the city's East End, where the Capitol Complex could have more room to expand.

As a photo in the December 18, 1921 edition of the *Gazette* indicated, two locations were primarily under consideration by then. One was the current site of the Capitol, which is east of downtown on the north side of the Kanawha River, while the other was across the river in the area where Charleston Area Medical Center's Memorial Hospital is located now. Gilbert favored the location on the south side of the river, which was known as the South Ruffner site. But in December 1921, the commission chose the East End location on the north side of the river, partly because it seemed to be cheaper and easier to build there and partly to avoid appearances of impropriety. Commission member Fred Staunton owned much land on the south side of the river, so if the commission had chosen the South Ruffner site, it would have raised suspicions of a deal to benefit him.

HOUSE MOVING

The chosen location was called the Duffy Street site, although the Capitol Complex eventually would eliminate Duffy Street when the campus expanded. Room to spread out was one of the reasons cited for building in the East End rather than downtown, but the land there was not empty. It was a residential neighborhood, so dozens of houses were in the way of the project. The state bought about fifty houses and was planning to tear them down, but some residents called for moving the houses instead. Despite some doubts about the feasibility of doing that, state officials let the homeowners repurchase their houses on the condition they would remove them from the site for the Capitol. They called on the John Eichleay Jr. Company of Pittsburgh to handle the moves in 1923. In an article published in the April 1925 edition of *American Magazine*, the head of the company, John P. Eichleay, said the firm had plenty of experience in moving not only houses but also an eight-story office building in Pittsburgh. But he said the Charleston project was one of the company's largest house-moving operations.

"The new sites of the houses were scattered over a considerable area, about a half-mile radius," Eichleay said. "One house had to go south, a second north, a third west, and so on, in every possible direction. Finally, all the houses were moved except twelve. All available lots in the district had been taken, and the question arose, 'What shall we do with these extra houses?'"

The Eichleay company suggested moving them to the south side of the river to "start a new town" over there.

> *Real estate men, eager to develop the other shore of the Kanawha, at once fell in with the plan, and we were told to go ahead... We brought down two steel barges from Pittsburgh, and hitched them together, with a wooden barge between. This time—because of the number of houses to be moved—we built a more or less permanent trestle of truss-work and cross-piling from the curb of the street to our platform of cribbing on the barges, a distance of 225 feet. Railroad tracks were laid on this, and over it, and without the least trouble the houses were drawn, one at a time, by a horse-power*

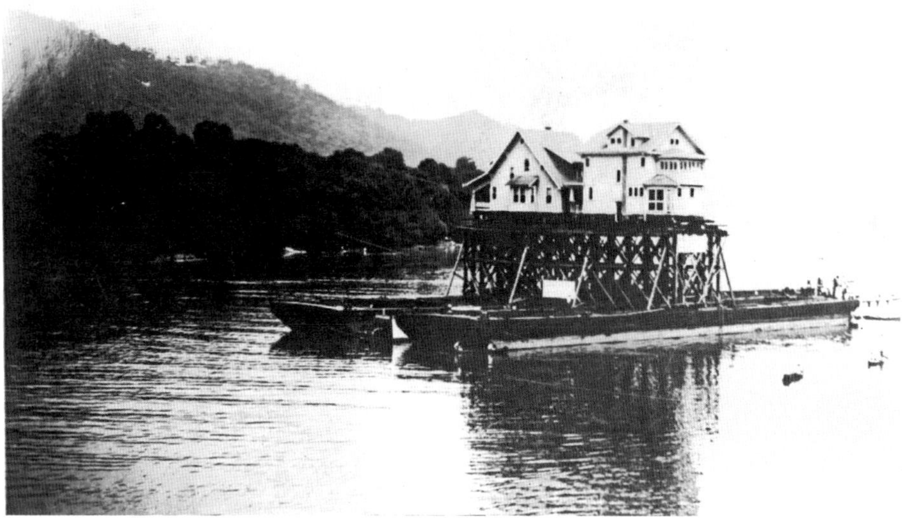

The John Eichleay Jr. Company of Pittsburgh moved about fifty houses from the property designated for the new Capitol in 1923. That included moving twelve of them, including these two, on barges across the Kanawha River. *Photo courtesy of Eichleay Engineers, Inc., of California, and the Detre Library and Archives, Heinz History Center, Pittsburgh.*

> *capstan. The barges took two houses a trip. Within three weeks we had the whole twelve relocated on the other side of the Kanawha.*

The clearing of the site changed Charleston's East End forever and prepared the state for a Capitol unlike any it ever had before.

Chapter 4

The Master's Plan

The architecture of the Capitol that burned in 1921 fit the Victorian style of the late nineteenth century when it was built, as did that of the building in Wheeling it had replaced. But Cass Gilbert reached back to Italian Renaissance architecture, which itself was based on the architecture of ancient Rome, when he drew up plans for the new Capitol. With few exceptions, today's Capitol is largely the structure that Gilbert designed in the 1920s. It is symmetrical in a U-shape with four-story wings on each side of the central section, which has porticos on the north and south sides and a dome in the middle. It is built largely of Indiana limestone and Imperial Danby Vermont marble.

The east and west wings are each 300 feet long and 60 feet wide. Between the windows on the upper three floors are pilasters that support the cornice. Each has a flat roof enclosed by a balustrade parapet, as does the Capitol's central section, which is 558 feet long and 120 feet wide.

Gilbert described the outside of the Capitol as "classic in style; in fact it might more correctly be termed Renaissance. The architectural forms are Roman, with the single exception of the Doric vestibule at the ground floor of the Main Building on the river side. The porticoes and the colonnades of the exterior are distinctly Roman, the two main porticoes being of the Roman Corinthian order, which was, of course, indirectly derived from the Greek precedent, and the other porticoes or colonnades are of a modified Roman Doric type."

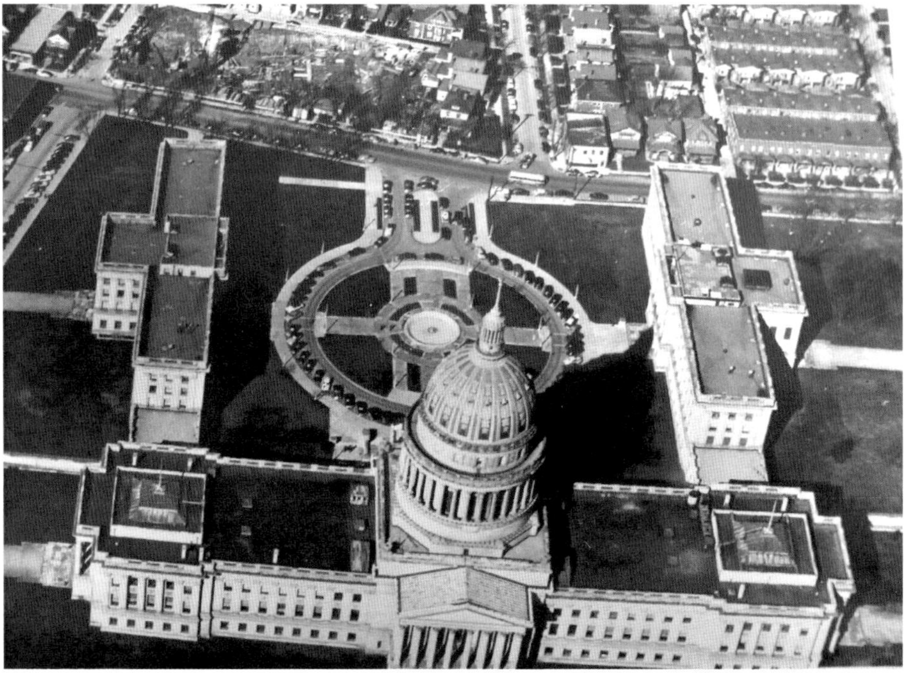

The U-shape of the Capitol can be seen in this aerial photo that was taken before other buildings were added to the campus. Washington Street still formed the northern boundary of the Capitol grounds, and Duffy Street (left) still existed on the western side. In those years, cars were allowed to park around the Capitol Circle. *Photo courtesy of Charleston Newspapers.*

DOME IS ESSENTIAL FEATURE

The dome is 292 feet high, which makes it more than 4 feet higher than the dome of the U.S. Capitol, although not as wide. It is crowned by a lantern, which is topped by a bronze staff on which a golden eagle is perched. Gilbert modeled the dome after one in Paris atop L'Hôtel National des Invalides (The National Residence of the Invalids), which contains the tomb of Napoleon Bonaparte as well as those of many other French leaders. Instead of French and Catholic heraldic emblems and a cross on top, Gilbert substituted American symbols such as flags on the panels and the eagle on top.

Of the exterior of the dome, Gilbert said, it "closely follows the Roman precedent, although, perhaps, there is no dome as high in proportion among Roman examples. The dome has become by habit and use as much a feature of the American State Capitol as the steeple is a feature of the American village Church, or the tower a feature of an English parliament building. The gilding on the dome brings out that graceful upward soaring quality, which gives it a large measure of its charm and beauty."

Slightly more than halfway up the dome, each panel has a little window. That is a feature that Gilbert seems to have copied from L'Hôtel National des Invalides in France, but a story passed down over many years contends that the windows in the West Virginia Capitol have a function other than mere decoration or to let light in. Tom Susman, a former legislator whose parents both served in the legislature, heard the story after he became acting secretary of the Department of Administration in April 2003. While he inspected damage to the dome, workers told him that if the Capitol ever came under siege, defenders could use the windows as gun turrets. As the story goes, when state officials commissioned the Capitol to be designed in the 1920s, memories of the mine wars of the preceding decade were still fresh, so the concept of using the Capitol as a fortress against enemies who might attempt to seize it was not far-fetched.

Under the blue vaulted ceiling of the dome is a rotunda with a circular-arched hall on the second floor. Hanging from the center of the dome is a two-ton chandelier of hand-cut Czechoslovakian crystal that is eight feet in diameter. The arches on the north and south sides open to the porticos, while those on the east and west sides open to foyers leading to the chambers for the Senate and the House of Delegates.

In the nomination form the state filed to get the Capitol listed on the National Register of Historic Places, the rotunda is described further:

> *The arches extend to the base of the dome and are adorned with lunette panels of deep-blue plaster. The floor of the rotunda, circular in plan around an open well, is inlaid with Italian travertine and white Vermont marble. A balustrade encircles the well in the rotunda floor, through which can be seen a colonnaded hall on the floor below. Gold-leaf bands decorate the walls of the circular drum and ceiling of the dome, which are in shades of blue, gray and old rose. A row of slender windows covered with gold-leaf grilles encircles the dome at the base of the bell.*

The same marble extends through the walls and floors of the foyers between the legislative chambers and the rotunda. The ceilings of the foyers are filled with square coffers, each one of which has a bronze cluster of leaves against a rose background. Along the walls, translucent Italian alabaster urns hold lights and are supported by standards of black and gold Belgian marble.

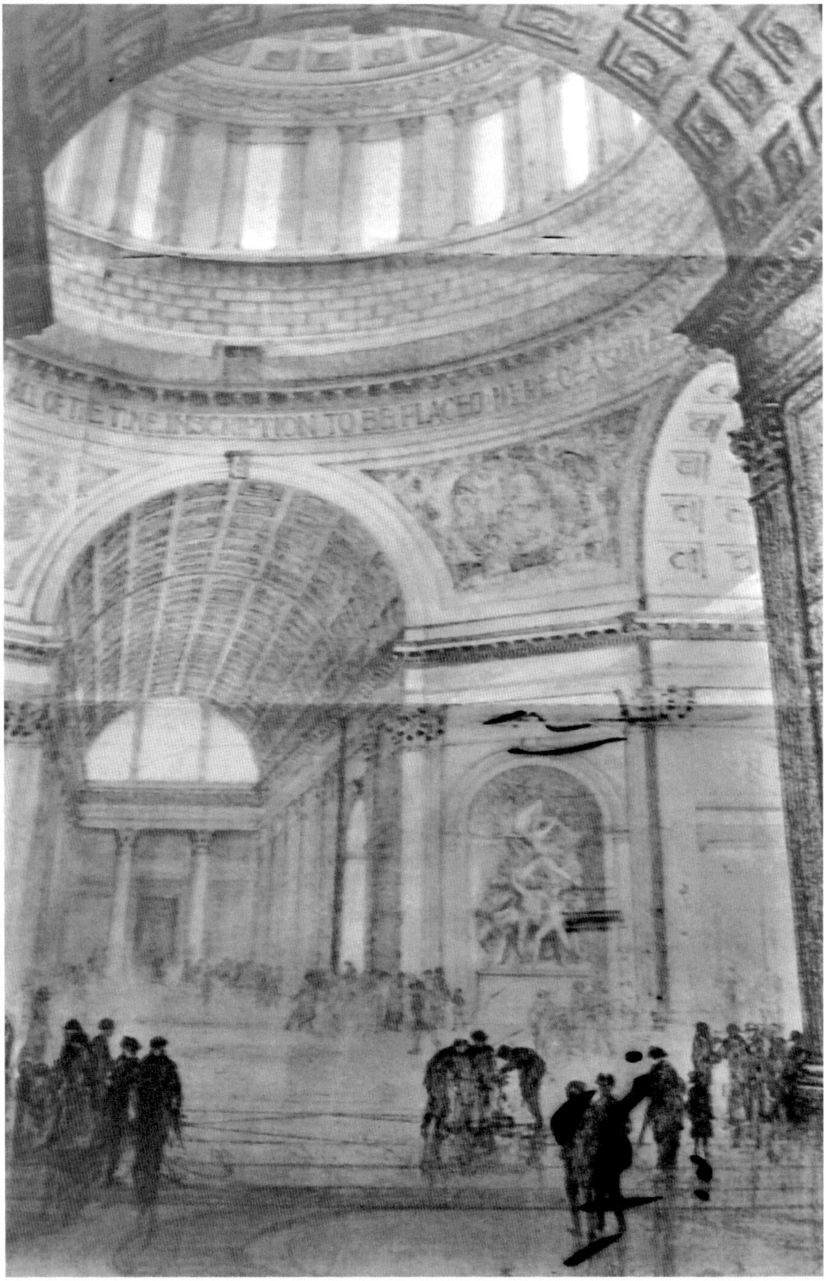

Architect Cass Gilbert made this sketch of what he wanted the rotunda of the Capitol to look like.

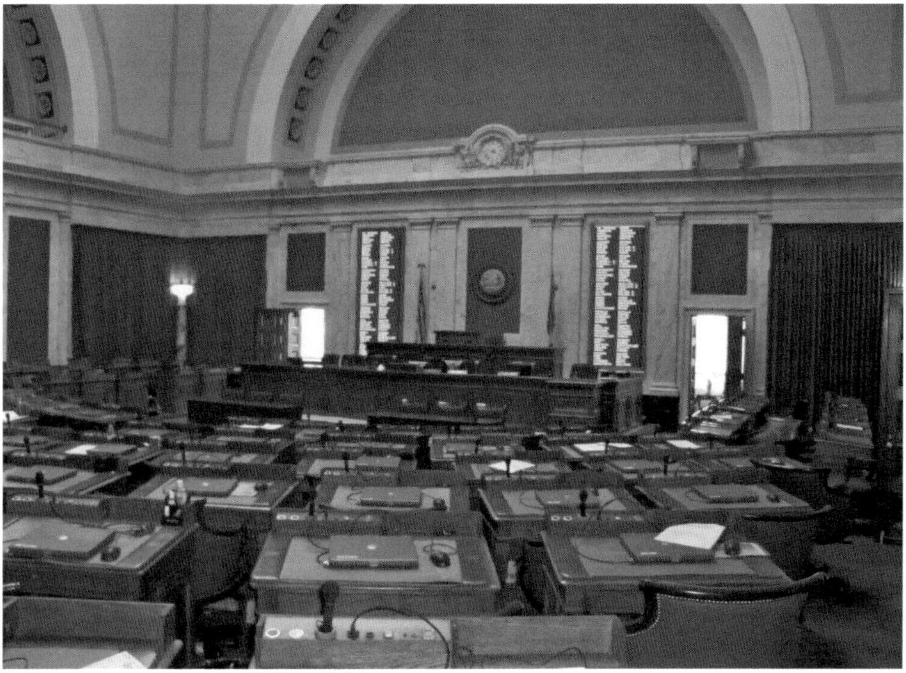

The House of Delegates chamber now accommodates one hundred members. *Photo by Jim Wallace.*

The House of Delegates chamber is at the end of the east foyer, and the Senate chamber is on the opposite side, both on the second floor. The chambers are similar, but the Senate must accommodate desks for only thirty-four members, while the House has one hundred, although in the 1920s, when Gilbert drew his plans, the Senate had just thirty members, and the House had just ninety-four. Each chamber has three public galleries framed by large arches that look down on the main floor. In the rear of each gallery is a small, arched window with ornamental bronze grilles. Under the fourth arch is the dais where the presiding officer stands and legislative staff members work. The domed ceiling has a small cupola with a stained-glass skylight. Hanging from a brass chain in the center is a chandelier of imported, hand-cut glass.

Although Gilbert has received much credit for designing a beautiful and functional Capitol, many visitors in recent years have wished that he had made legislative committee rooms larger. The House Finance and Judiciary committee rooms, in particular, seem especially inadequate when lobbyists and other observers try to squeeze into seats along the walls, because the

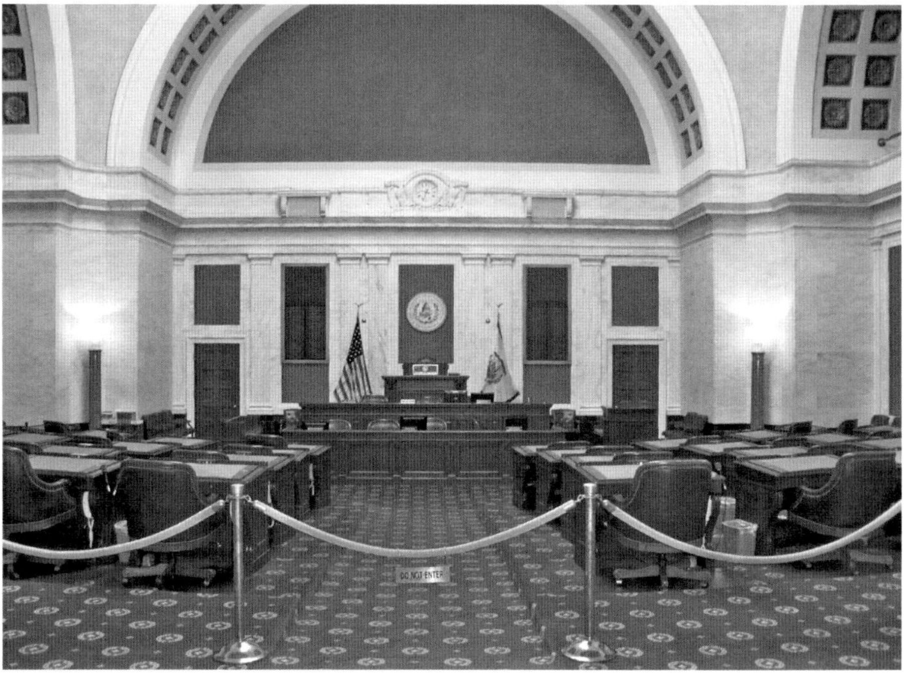

The Senate chamber is similar to the House chamber but accommodates only thirty-four members. *Photo by Jim Wallace.*

tables where legislators sit take up most of the space. But Tom Susman, who served in the House from 1987 through 1992 and spent many more years as a lobbyist, said Gilbert should not be blamed.

"The original committee rooms were not designed for the public," he said. "They were designed for the members and their invited guests. They would lock the doors when they started committee meetings." That changed as government began opening to more public scrutiny in the 1970s after the Watergate scandal in Washington, D.C., brought down President Richard Nixon, Susman said.

Several stairways connect the first and second floors of the central unit of the Capitol, but the grandest are a pair of white marble stairways on the south side of the rotunda. The ground floor is a hall with fluted Doric columns with six crystal lights suspended on bronze chains. A circular colonnade with sixteen square Doric piers that enclose the rotunda well is in the center. Inside the colonnade are pairs of bronze light stands.

The governor's suite of offices is in the southwestern corner of the ground floor of the building. The one room open to the public is the reception room,

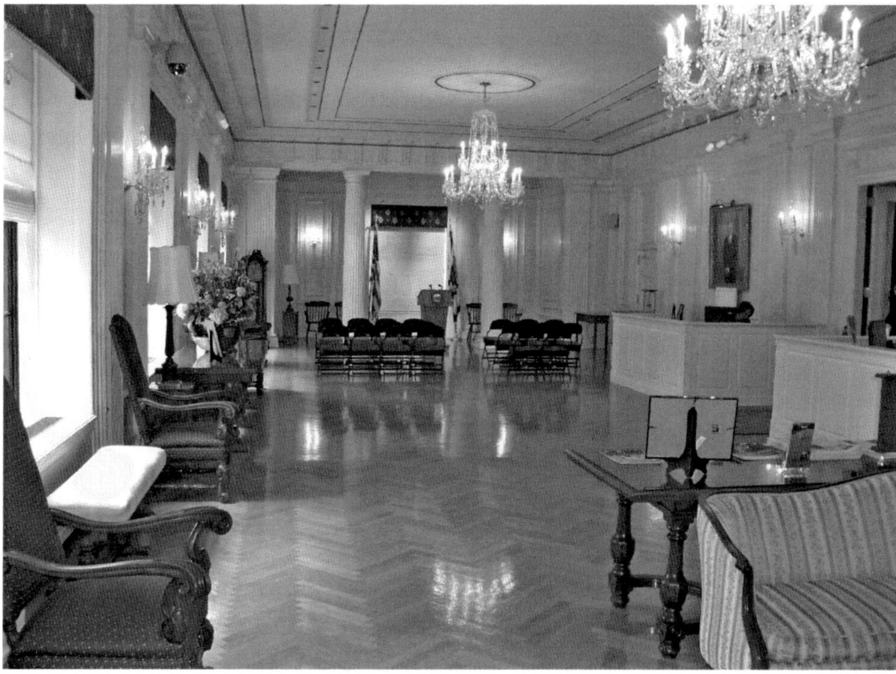

The reception room of the governor's office often is used for news conferences and public ceremonies. *Photo by Jim Wallace.*

which, like the nearby Governor's Mansion, is Georgian Colonial–style. It has ivory walls with fluted Corinthian pilasters. The parquet floor has a herringbone pattern and a border of quarter-sawed oak, black walnut and maple. At the eastern end of the room, closest to the door to the governor's inner office, is a fireplace made of black and gold Belgian marble. Two large, crystal chandeliers hang from the ceiling and are complemented by crystal wall brackets around the room.

Other ground floor offices in the main unit of the Capitol are those for the secretary of state and the attorney general. The auditor has offices on the ground floor of the west wing, and the treasurer has offices on the ground floor of the east wing. The legislature has offices and meeting rooms on the second floor of both wings, as well as on the upper floors of the central unit. The House also has some first-floor offices. Plans are for legislators to take more office space in the wings after the offices of the auditor and treasurer are moved into Building 3 of the Capitol Complex following the renovation of that building.

But for decades after the Capitol opened, most legislators did not have office space. A delegate or senator who was not in a leadership position had only a desk in the House or Senate chamber and a filing cabinet in the hallway. Tom Susman, who served in the House from 1987 through 1992, recalled that his father, Alan Susman, who was a senator in the 1970s, had to get a leadership position before he got a Capitol office, and even then, he had to share it with two other senators. "When I came in, they started giving delegates offices, and we shared them with four different delegates," Tom Susman said.

Susman also recalled that document safes were located throughout the Capitol. "They were put in there because the other buildings [the 1885 Capitol and the "Pasteboard Capitol"] burned down, and all the documents were lost," he said. "So there were all kinds of document safes with locked doors [in the current Capitol]." Many of those safes were removed late in the twentieth century and early in the twenty-first century after backing up records on computers became a standard practice, Susman said.

The chamber and offices for the Supreme Court of Appeals are located on the third floor of the east wing. The chamber is forty feet by forty-four feet with a ceiling that is thirty feet high. At the top is a rectangular skylight with stained glass. On the sides of the skylight, bronze carvings depict the book of law and a scale and balance. A frieze that runs along the top of the walls contains quotations from two U.S. presidents. From Thomas Jefferson: "The true foundation of republican government is the equal right of every citizen in his person and property and in their management." From Abraham Lincoln: "Firmness in the right as God gives us to see the right."

The walls of the Supreme Court's chamber are made of white Imperial Danby Vermont marble. On the sides and front of the chamber are columns of the same marble on bases of black Belgian marble. Behind the columns are burgundy drapes. The justices sit behind a long bench of American walnut. Chairs and other furniture are made of the same wood. The original floor was made of compressed cork, but dark red carpet has covered it for many years.

Cass Gilbert liked the design of the chamber so much that he used it as the basis for the chamber of the United States Supreme Court, which was his final major project before his death.

Not only did Gilbert use Roman-style architecture on the Capitol, but he also made sure that visitors to the building would be greeted by Roman gods and goddesses, who were generally the same as Greek gods and goddesses but usually with different names. Arched entrances on the east side and west side of the main unit of the Capitol have busts of three Roman deities each looking out above them. Likewise, entrances from the north-side courtyard to the east

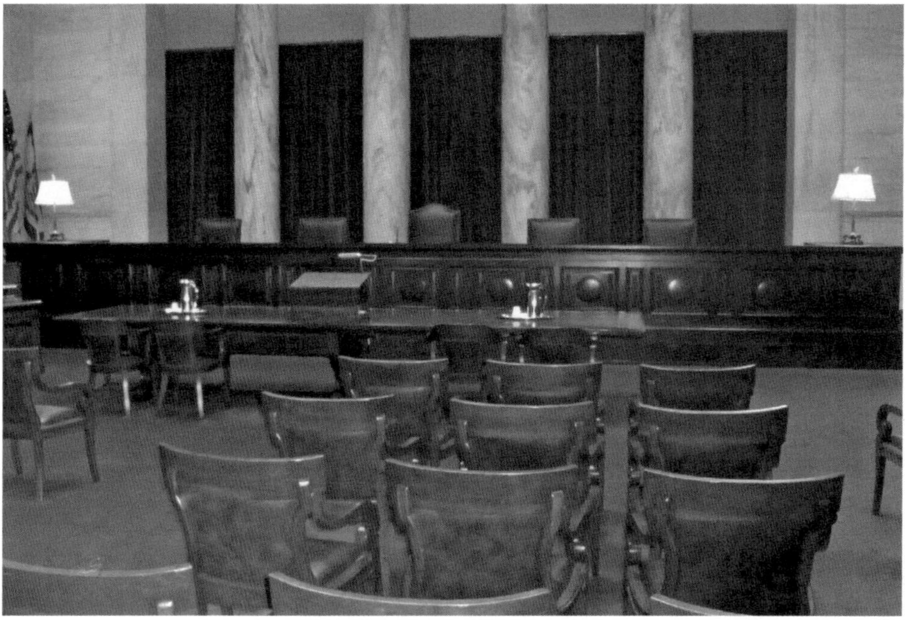

Cass Gilbert based his later design of the United States Supreme Court chamber on this chamber he designed for the West Virginia Supreme Court of Appeals. *Photo by Jim Wallace.*

and west wings also have three such busts each. A skilled sculptor carved the busts out of limestone blocks after they were installed on the building.

People entering the west side of the main unit, as the governor would when coming from the Governor's Mansion, see the busts of Vesta (Hestia in Greek), Neptune (Poseidon) and Ceres (Demeter), as viewed from left to right. Vesta was the goddess of the hearth and home, as well as the protector of the sacred flame. Neptune was the god of the sea, as well as horses. The eighth planet from the sun bears his name. Ceres is the goddess of earth and agriculture. A dwarf planet that is the largest body in the asteroid belt between Mars and Jupiter is named for Ceres.

People who enter the west wing from the courtyard on the northern side of the Capitol are greeted by Fortuna (Tyche), Jupiter (Zeus) and Hercules (Heracles). Fortuna was the goddess of luck or chance. Jupiter was king of the gods, as well as god of the sky. The fifth planet from the sun, and the largest in the solar system, is named for him. Hercules, a half-god whose father was Jupiter and whose mother was a mortal, accomplished a series of twelve heroic tasks, or labors. He is memorialized as a northern constellation, which can be seen almost overhead at times on summer evenings.

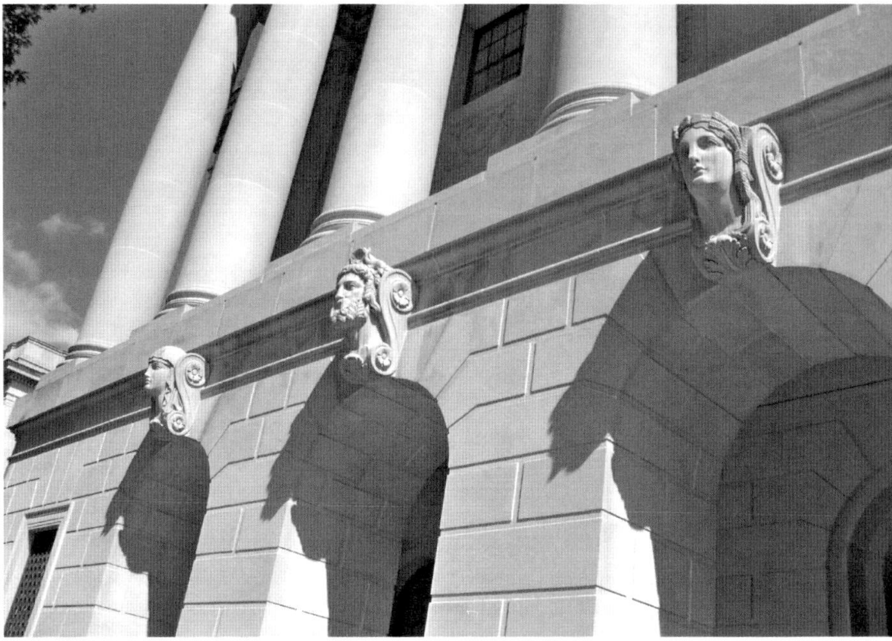

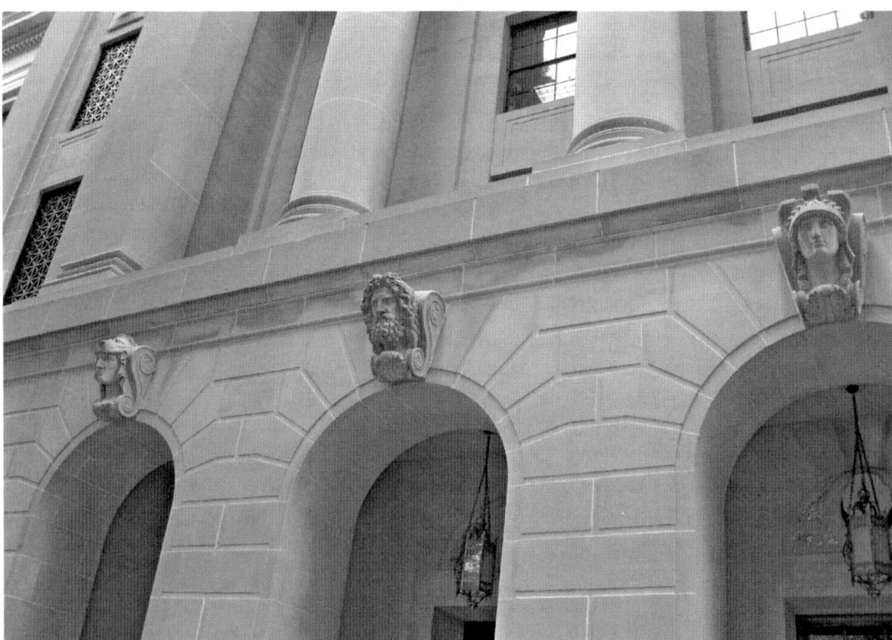

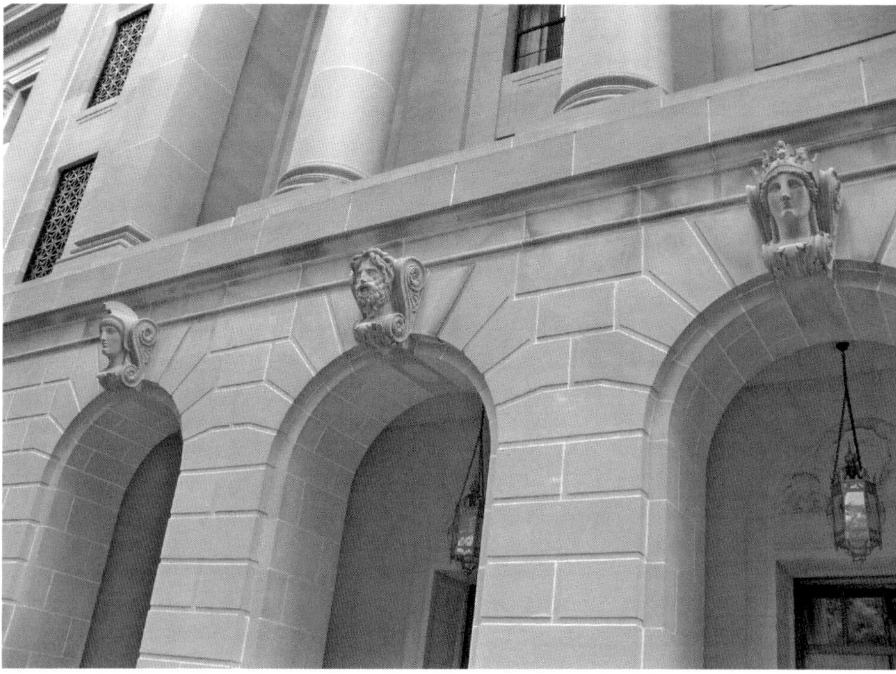

Above: Busts of Juno, Prometheus and Perseus are found on the entrance to the east wing from the courtyard. *Photo by Jim Wallace.*

Opposite top: Busts of Vesta, Neptune and Ceres greet visitors entering the Capitol from the west side. *Photo by Jim Wallace.*

Opposite bottom: The west wing's courtyard entrance features the busts of Fortuna, Jupiter and Hercules. *Photo by Jim Wallace.*

On the opposite side of the courtyard, the entrance to the east wing features Juno (Hera), Prometheus and Perseus. Juno was queen of the deities, wife to Jupiter and goddess of women and marriage. Prometheus (same name for Romans and Greeks) was the god who gave humans the gift of fire. He was punished by Jupiter by being chained to a rock and having his liver eaten by an eagle. Perseus (same name for Romans and Greeks) was the son of Jupiter and the hero who slayed a monster and the snake-haired Medusa and then married Andromeda. He is commemorated in a constellation that can be seen in the northeastern part of the sky on autumn evenings.

At the entrance to the east side of the Capitol's main unit are the busts of Mercury (Hermes), Vulcan (Hephaestus) and Minerva (Athena). Mercury was the son of Jupiter and a protector of such diverse groups of humans as

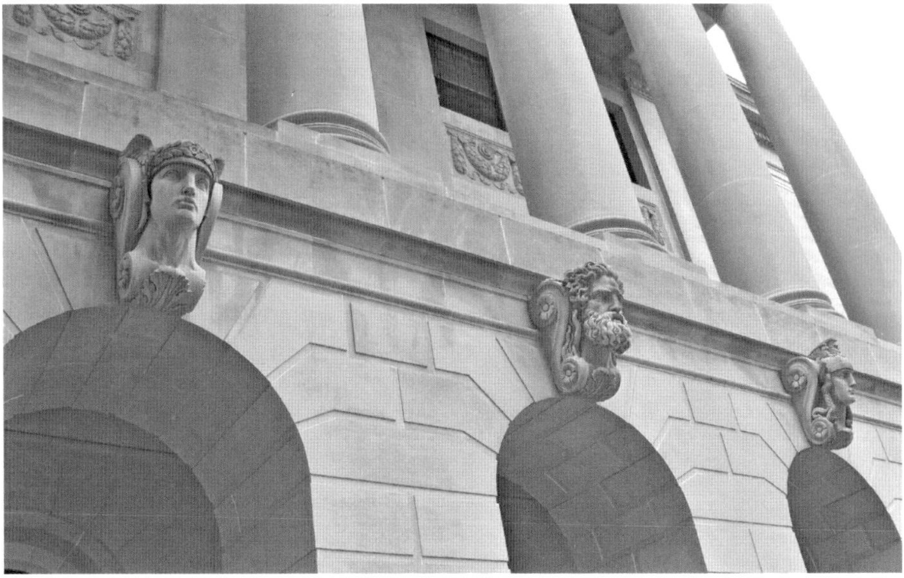

When people enter the east side of the Capitol's main unit, they pass under the busts of Mercury, Vulcan and Minerva. *Photo by Jim Wallace.*

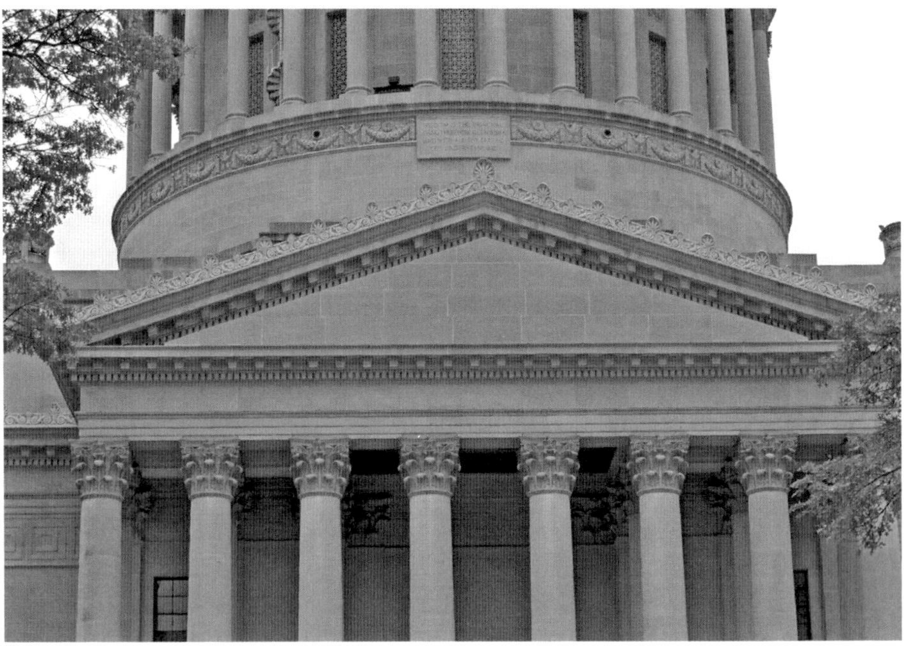

The pediment above the south portico of the Capitol remains blank despite Cass Gilbert's desire to have it filled with sculpture. *Photo by Jim Wallace.*

shepherds, travelers and thieves. He was also a messenger of the gods and is depicted with wings on his cap. The planet that bears his name is closest to the sun and thus the one that travels the fastest in its orbit. Vulcan, a son of Jupiter and Juno, was the god of fire. Minerva was the goddess of wisdom, as well as handicrafts and eventually warfare. She sprung fully grown and armored from the head of Jupiter.

Yet even with such adornments, the Capitol remains incomplete, at least in terms of fulfilling Gilbert's vision. He wanted the pediments—the triangular sections above the columns on the main north and south porticos—to be filled with sculpture. He called that "essential to the completion of the exterior design." However, the pediments remain blank. Likewise, Gilbert said, "Mural decorations of an adequate character should embellish the rotunda and the House and Senate, and in the reception rooms and corridors surrounding the House and Senate chambers there should be reasonably modest but adequate decorative treatment." Although the ceilings of the first-floor corridors of the two wings have murals, the state has yet to put them in the other locations where Gilbert wanted them.

Just completing construction of the Capitol in the midst of the Great Depression was enough of an accomplishment that the finishing touches of sculptures and murals were easy to put off. Gilbert's high standards for the work also could have put off state officials:

> *The sculpture and mural decorations should be done under proper guidance and direction and by artists of established reputation and experience and of real ability. There is nothing so valueless as poor art and nothing so ephemeral as passing fashion in art; therefore what is to be done should be done by competent and serious artists of proved ability and in accordance with the highest standards of good taste. The architect who develops the design is the best qualified to select the artists and experts who would carry it out sympathetically. It is the only way in which a consistent result can be obtained. Without this there will be intrusion of incidental sculpture and decorations in questionable taste.*

Almost eighty years after Gilbert wrote those words, the Manchin administration came closer than any other administration to having the murals painted. The process got as far in 2010 as having representatives from seven art studios from West Virginia, Ohio, New York, Wisconsin and Oregon participate in a pre-bid conference for a contract to paint the murals. The administration had hoped to have the murals completed in 2011 or early 2012 in the main rotunda and the smaller, first-floor rotundas near the governor's and attorney general's offices. But by the time the administration had planned to award a contract late that summer, Joe Manchin was involved in a campaign for the U.S. Senate seat of the late Robert Byrd, and he left the governor's office that fall. Rob Ferguson, who served as secretary of the Department of Administration from 2005 until 2012, said finances also got in the way. "The budget indicated that we were looking perhaps at some austere times in the future, so it got mothballed," he said.

Despite the lack of such final touches, the people who have worked in the Capitol over several decades and those responsible for maintaining it have kept Gilbert's designs in high regard, sometimes to the point of reverence. For example, the application for the National Register of Historic Places stated: "Gilbert's idea of combining the best materials with consideration of function and cost led to construction of an edifice which would be as practical as it was beautiful."

Gilbert also urged state officials to put terraces and landscaping around the Capitol. In a letter to Governor Conley, he called them "essential features of the design" and noted that they had been included in all the approved designs and published illustrations of the project.

"I mention these features at this time as indicating that this phase of the project is not an additional one but merely carries to completion that which was originally contemplated," Gilbert wrote. He added that leaving them out would be equivalent to leaving the Capitol "without cornices or porticos."

Further, Gilbert urged the state to acquire additional land so the Capitol would have "more ample grounds" for state government. "Sooner or later the surrounding location will be in demand for higher buildings than at the present time, and the probability is that the State Capitol will be dominated by private structures which would obviously be undesirable if the property is not controlled by the State," he wrote.

Over the years, state government did acquire more land around the Capitol and landscaped it, although not entirely as Gilbert envisioned it.

Chapter 5

Construction

The construction of the new Capitol was a taxing project, not only for the workers involved but also for West Virginia citizens, because in 1921, the legislature approved a gross sales tax to come up with funding. Money for the project also came from the sale of the former downtown Capitol grounds for about $1.5 million, sale of the Capitol Annex for about $500,000, sale of the grounds of the temporary Capitol and the old governor's mansion for more than $350,000, insurance payments for the old Capitol and its contents of more than $500,000 and the sale of several houses on the site of the new Capitol for more than $100,000. Kanawha County also gave the state $1 million for the Capitol, perhaps to ensure it would be built in Charleston and not somewhere else in the state.

Three for One

Although the final product was one large building, the Capitol was built in three units: first the west wing, then the east wing and finally the main unit that connected them. Each was treated as a separate project in terms of contracting, financing and construction. The state awarded contracts for the west wing on December 22, 1923. The George A. Fuller Company got the general construction contract. The groundbreaking ceremony was held on January 7, 1924.

The workers used a spur of track from the New York Central Railroad that curved onto the campus from near California Avenue to bring huge cranes and other equipment, as well as carloads of structural steel, limestone, marble and other materials, to the site. They laid 1,500 yards of concrete for the foundation and built the steel superstructure above it. On May 1, 1924, they laid the cornerstone. Construction of the west wing was finished in March 1925. It cost $1,218,171.32 and provided eighty-four thousand square feet of floor space.

Several state agencies soon moved into the building. They included offices for the auditor, bank commissioner, tax commissioner, Game and Fish Commission, Department of Mines, Department of Health, Department of Workmen's Compensation, the Board of Control and the superintendent of free schools. The treasurer's office also was scheduled to go into the west wing, but W.S. Johnson, the treasurer, rejected his accommodations. He thought the large safe in it lacked the security necessary for holding state records and money, especially considering how prevalent bank robberies were in those days. Gilbert initially balked at providing the secure facility Johnson requested, fearing that it would increase building costs by hundreds of thousands of dollars. But the Capitol Building Commission turned to experts on the construction of banks and learned that accommodating Johnson would cost only about $30,000. The commission arranged to put that more secure facility into the east wing.

Meanwhile, the state Prohibition Department, the agriculture commissioner and the State Police made a house that was still standing at the time on the Capitol grounds their temporary headquarters.

Second Wing

For more than a year, the west wing stood by itself. Then in 1926, the legislature made a new appropriation for construction of its twin, the east wing. The James Baird Company got the contract to build it, and work started in July 1926. The cornerstone was laid on November 30, 1926. But although the east wing was mainly a mirror image of the west wing on the outside, it had some key differences on the inside that required more time to build. It took until January 1928 for the east wing to be ready for occupancy.

Among the differences in the east wing were the security provisions for the treasurer's office. They included a vault that is ten feet high, seventeen

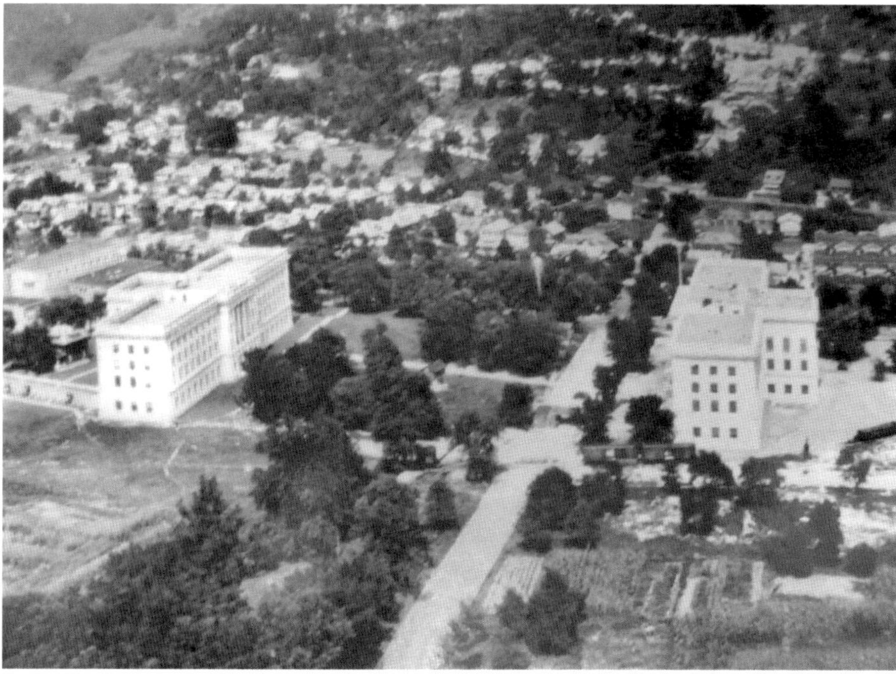

The west wing and east wing stood by themselves for two years before construction on the Capitol's main unit began.

feet long and twelve feet wide. It has a door made of solid steel that is fifteen inches thick with a weight of about fifteen tons. Surrounding the vault are eighteen-inch-thick, steel-reinforced walls. But in case that is not secure enough, the room containing the vault has three layers of half-inch steel in its walls, floor and ceiling. Inside the vault are forty separate safes, and each one has a double combination.

Also unlike the west wing, the east wing includes the Supreme Court chamber, which is two stories tall with its entrance on the third floor and its ceiling centered around a skylight on the roof. The chamber was a special project within the overall Capitol project for Cass Gilbert, who devoted personal attention to designing the décor and furnishings. The total cost of the east wing was $1,361,425.00.

In addition to the Supreme Court and the treasurer's office, state agencies that moved into the east wing in 1928 were the Road Commission, the Department of Agriculture and the Public Service Commission. In June 1929, the Department of Archives and History joined them there. That opened space in the Capitol Annex downtown for the Bureau of Labor, the

Board of Children's Guardians and the adjutant general's office. However, by that time, ownership of the annex had changed hands, and it had become the Charleston Library.

The state could have used the east wing several months before it was ready. Fire destroyed the "Pasteboard Capitol" on March 2, 1927. It began about 2:30 p.m. on the second floor. The fire spread rapidly, and the cause was never determined, but officials suggested most of the building might have been saved if water pressure and connections for emergency hoses had been better. Fortunately, only the Public Service Commission, the Road Commission and the Workmen's Compensation Department were still using the temporary Capitol at that time. By then, other agencies had moved to the west wing of the new Capitol, the Capitol Annex or other locations.

MAIN UNIT

Back at the new Capitol campus on the East End, the west wing and the east wing stood by themselves with nothing to connect them for more than two years. The legislature and the Capitol Building Commission exercised great care in spending money. They held off from starting a new phase of the project until the previous phase was completed and the bills were paid. For the main unit of the Capitol, lawmakers on March 2, 1929, approved a new tax of five cents per $100 of property valuation and established a Capitol Building Fund for the revenue. They also gave the commission and the governor permission to enter into a contract to build the main unit and spend up to $5 million. The commission then took until January 1930 to approve the architect's plans and seek bids for construction. Once again, the George A. Fuller Company got the contract, and construction began on March 6, 1930.

If state officials had realized early in 1929 that the United States was just months away from entering the Great Depression, they might have been more wary about proceeding with a multi-million-dollar building project. By the time construction began, more than four months had passed since the stock market crash, but the project went forward nevertheless. When officials held the ceremony to set the cornerstone on November 5, 1930, the Depression was a little more than one year old. Of course, the project came along at a good time for employees of more than forty companies that were subcontractors.

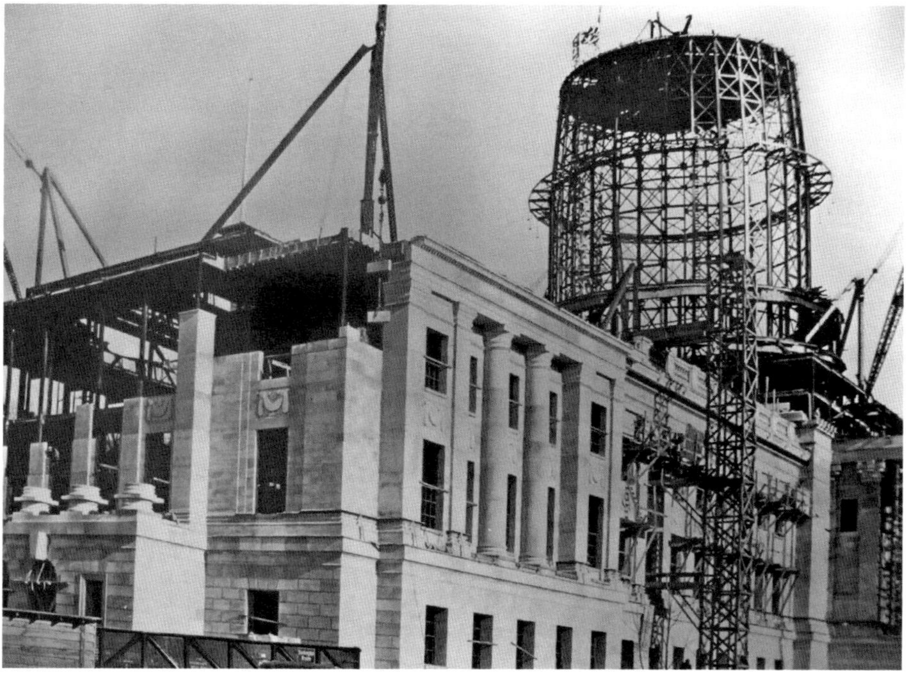

Construction of the Capitol's main unit, as shown in this 1931 photo, was not intended to be one of the public works projects providing employment during the Great Depression, but it turned out to be. *Photo courtesy of Charleston Newspapers.*

Some West Virginians thought the new Capitol was too extravagant, but not architect Cass Gilbert. In a letter he wrote to Walter Clark, editor of the *Charleston Daily Mail,* in 1932, Gilbert deplored extravagance and "unwise expenditure," but he maintained that the Capitol was neither:

> *People of modest means cannot afford to embellish their homes with works of art and a reasonable function of the State in the direction of culture and education, and in the development of civilization, is to provide in the State Capitol, which is owned and used by all of the people, suitable decorations of idealistic character, and the expenditure necessary for doing it is justified.*

FIRST BATTLE OF THE DOME

Of all the features of the Capitol, the dome seemed to be the primary target of critics who disagreed with Gilbert about what was extravagant. His plan to cover the outside of the dome with gold leaf while the nation was in the depths of the Depression struck them as improper. But Gilbert explained that it really would be cheaper than the alternative. "If we had built the dome of stone, as in the Arkansas state capitol, or of marble as in the Minnesota state capitol or the Rhode Island state capitol, it would have cost five or ten times as much money and probably would not have excited any comment whatever," Gilbert said in a newspaper article.

His estimate was that a marble dome of the same dimension would have cost at least $500,000. However, Gilbert said, "the comparatively modest expense for covering it with newly developed material of lead coated with copper and using gilding has reduced the cost to a minimum." He cited the capitols of New Jersey and Massachusetts, as well as the Library of Congress in Washington, D.C, as examples of other public buildings with gilded domes. Further, Gilbert argued that maintenance costs for a gilded dome would be lower. He said that "if the bell of the dome were of limestone it would be, in that climate, susceptible to expansion and contraction and the joints would have to be constantly repaired in order to preserve it."

Some critics suggested that painting the dome would be cheaper, but Gilbert rejected that option. Repainting the metal dome would be necessary every two or three years, he said, so eventually it would be more expensive than applying gold leaf. In response to the specific suggestion of painting the dome the same gray as the Capitol's limestone, he said it would be "a cheap pretense of being stone, and the painting would have cost at least $12,000." Gilbert also dismissed another proposal to leave the dome uncoated and let the copper show. He said doing so "would lose entirely that graceful upward soaring quality which gives it a large measure of its charm and beauty."

Gilbert got his way: The Mack, Jenny and Tyler Company of New York gilded the dome in 1931 for $23,700. It didn't stay that way forever, but initially at least, the dome was golden.

Along with constructing the main unit, the builders had to connect it to the two wings with 95-foot-long sections that are one story high on top of basements and 56 feet wide. The main unit itself is 558 feet long and 120 feet wide. One year after construction began, most of the exterior of the main unit was completed, although the steel framework of the dome was still going up and the railroad spur still ran through where the connector to

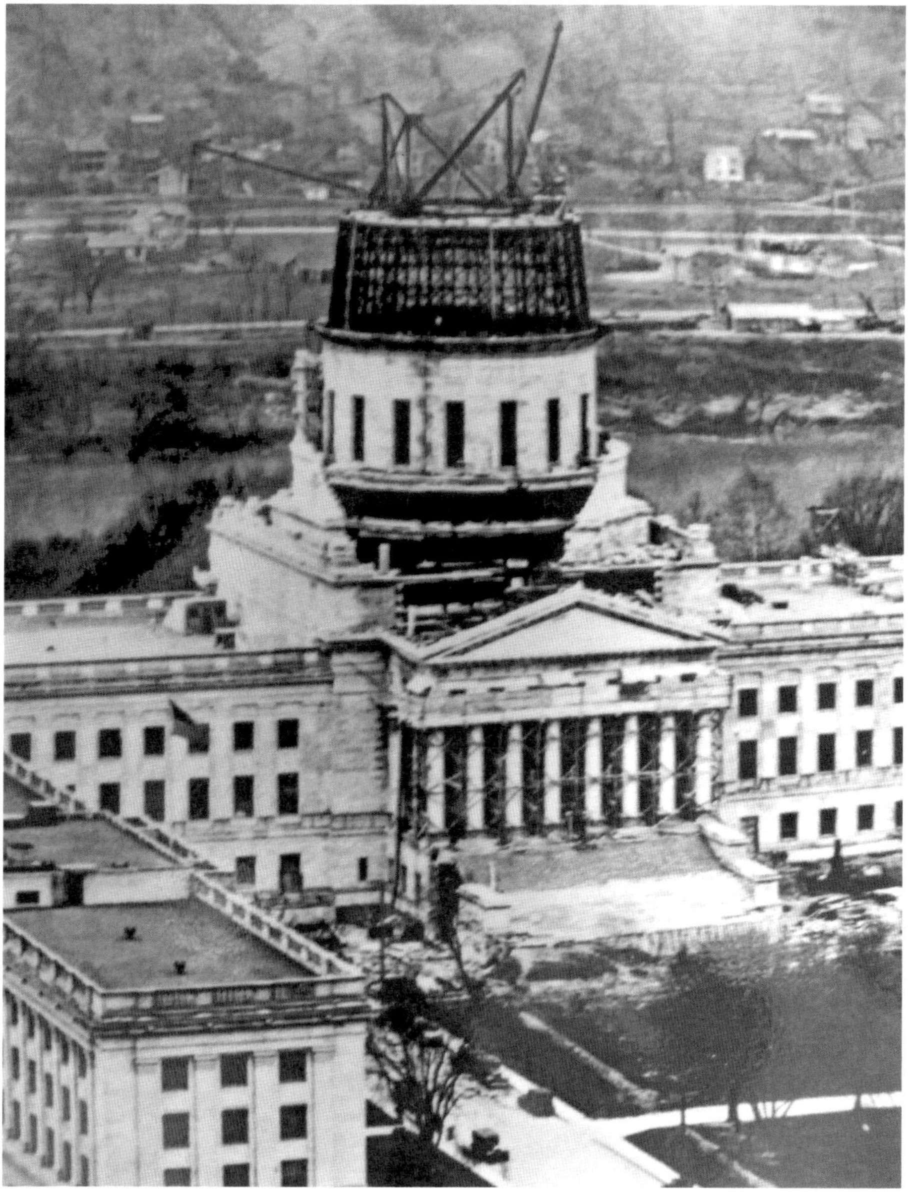

About a year's worth of construction remained when this photo was taken of the Capitol. *Photo courtesy of Charleston Newspapers.*

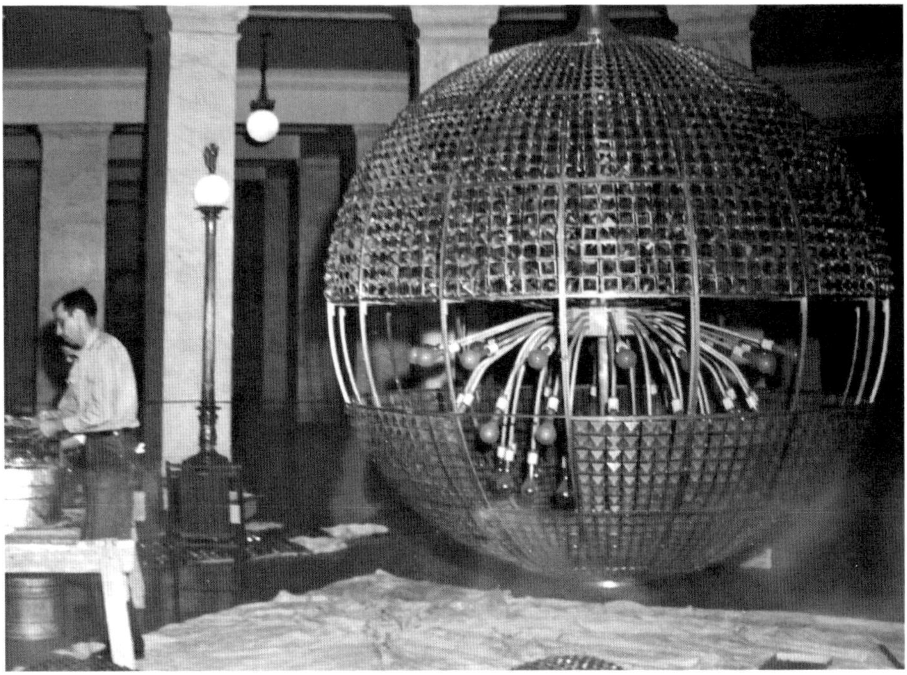

Workers put together the Czechoslovakian chandelier in the rotunda in 1932. *Photo courtesy of Kanawha County Public Library.*

the east wing was being built. By early 1932, the main unit was ready to be used. The Capitol received its formal dedication on West Virginia Day, June 20, 1932, when the state was sixty-nine years old, in a ceremony held on the north portico.

AMONG NATION'S BEST

Although Gilbert could not attend the dedication, in his letter to Clark, he referred to the design as "noble and distinguished simplicity." Further, he wrote:

> *Simplicity and good proportion, which are finer characteristics than ornamentation, have been carried out in the rotunda and the principal corridors, and in the rooms of the House and Senate especially, an air of simplicity, amplitude and dignity has been achieved. While not extravagant*

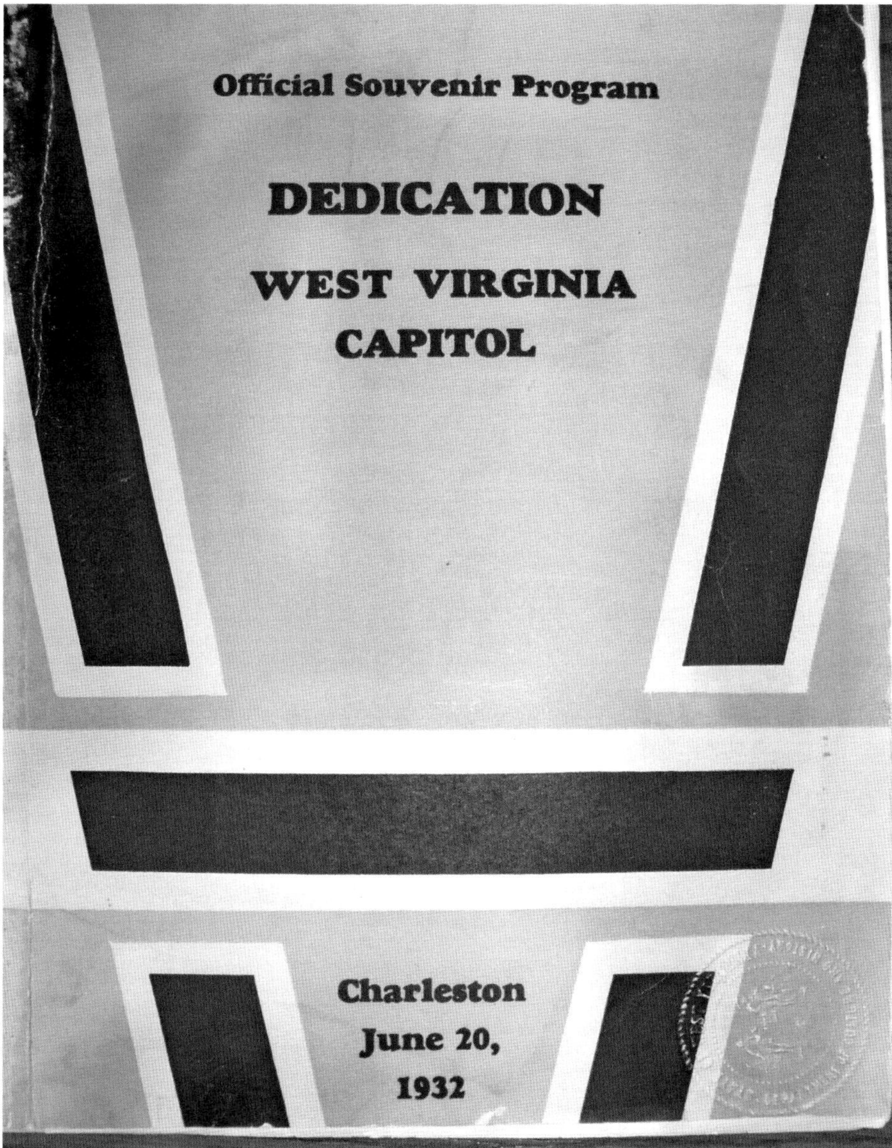

People who attended the dedication of the Capitol received a blue-and-gold souvenir program.

> *or elaborate in detail or material, nevertheless it can properly take its place as among the best buildings in the United States.*

In a personal message Gilbert wrote for publication in the *Charleston Gazette,* he noted that the Capitol was "well built and the cost is well within the amount appropriated by the legislature and very much less than was originally proposed by the state."

Construction of the main unit of the Capitol cost $4,482,623.21, which was more than $500,000.00 less than the $5,000,000.00 authorized by the legislature. The total cost for building the Capitol, including acquisition of the property and landscaping, was $9,491,180.03. However, the official souvenir program for the Capitol's dedication placed the net cost to taxpayers at just $6,412,373.60. That calculation resulted from deducting $1,551,000 for sale of the former Capitol's site downtown, $501,236.59 for sale of the Capitol Annex, $352,223.84 for sale of the site of the "Pasteboard Capitol" and the former Governor's Mansion, $533,455.23 for insurance settlements on the old buildings and their contents, $104,586.52 for sale of houses that had stood on the site of the new Capitol and $36,284.25 for interest received on deferred payments.

The project spanned the terms of three governors: Ephraim Morgan (1921–25), Howard Gore (1925–29) and William Conley (1929–33). Beginning in March 1933, Herman Kump became the first governor to serve in the completed Capitol throughout his term.

Chapter 6

The Mansions

Two mansions sit at the southwestern corner of the Capitol Complex. The newer one plays an active role in the political and cultural life of the state. The other has a longer history but an uncertain future.

FIRST GOVERNOR'S MANSION

The job of governor comes with much responsibility but also with some nice benefits. One is having a handsome office in the Capitol. Another is having a spacious home provided by taxpayers and a short commute to work.

Since 1893, the state has provided a residence for the governor and his family. Before then, each governor had to provide for his own housing. The last governor who had to do that was Aretas Fleming. As his term neared an end in 1893, he made this recommendation to the legislature:

> *The state should provide a suitable house at the seat of government for the use of the governor during his term of office. The law requires the governor to reside at the capital, and in order to do so, he must either pay high rents or purchase property that must usually be sold at a sacrifice when his term of office expires. The salary paid the governor is comparatively small, and he should be relieved of the necessity of*

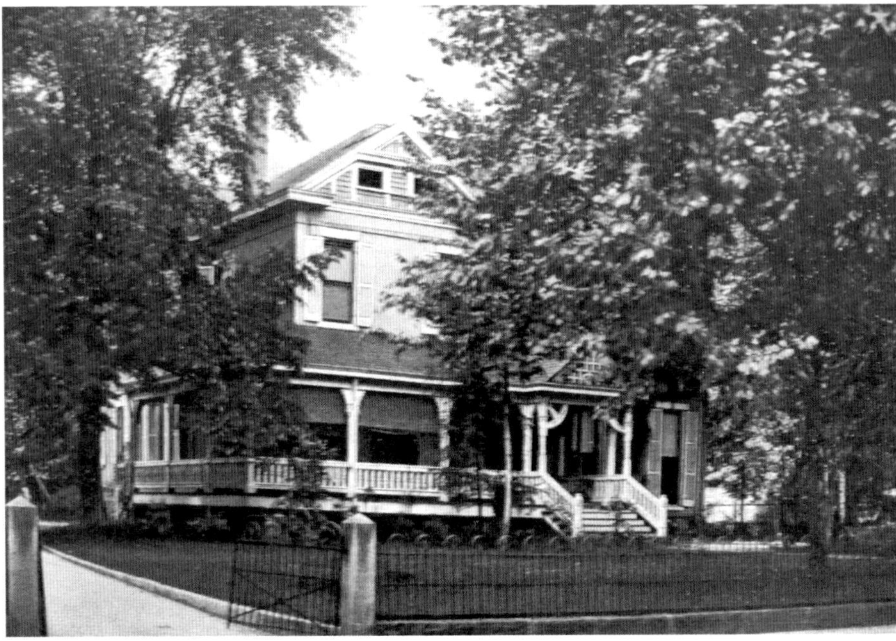

The first Governor's Mansion, seen in this early twentieth-century postcard, was located on Capitol Street near the old Capitol.

> *incurring expense or loss about this matter. I therefore recommend that an appropriation be made at least for the purchase of suitable grounds upon which to erect an executive mansion. Any appropriation so made should be from the revenue of 1893-94.*

Lawmakers took Fleming's advice, but instead of building a home for the governor, the state bought a mansion that already was located conveniently at 153 Capitol Street diagonally across from the Capitol. The Jelenko brothers, who were in the wholesale dry goods business, built the house about 1890. The state bought it for $22,000. It was a white, wooden, Queen Anne–style house with two stories. It had a large front porch that wrapped part of the way around one side.

William MacCorkle, who succeeded Fleming in 1893, was the first of eight governors to live in the mansion. He later built his own mansion, Sunrise, overlooking downtown Charleston on a hill south of the Kanawha River.

SECOND GOVERNOR'S MANSION

After the Capitol burned down in 1921, state officials decided not only to build a new Capitol but also a new home for governors. Although the Capitol Building Commission did not choose the location for the new Capitol until December 20, 1921, the location for the Governor's Mansion was chosen half a year earlier. On July 7, 1921, the state paid $64,270 for three parcels in Charleston's East End. That might have been an indication that the so-called Duffy Street site next to it already was favored as the location for the Capitol, because if any other location had been chosen for the Capitol, it would have required more than a brief stroll for governors to get to work.

Although Cass Gilbert received the contract to design the new Capitol, the commission turned to Walter Martens, a Charleston architect, to design the Governor's Mansion, or as it is formally known, the Executive Mansion. Martens consulted with Gilbert in New York to ensure that the mansion would complement the Capitol. Both of them sketched their concepts for the building and were pleased to find they were very similar. They chose a Georgian Colonial style.

Construction began in 1924 with the Wallace Knight Construction Company as the main contractor. The mansion is located just west of the Capitol and faces Kanawha Boulevard and the Kanawha River. As the state's application to the National Register of Historic Places described it, the mansion is built "of red Harvard colonial brick laid in Flemish bond with black headers. The Georgian Colonial building is fronted by a central, two-story portico with a bracketed pediment supported by four free standing and two engaged fluted Corinthian columns. The capitals of these columns are ornate with acanthus leaves, and this lends an impressive grace and dignity to the front of the mansion. The arched entranceway, painted white to complement the brickwork as is all trim, frames a delicate fanlight above the door."

Inside the front entrance, the reception foyer floor has a black-and-white checkerboard pattern. The black is Belgian marble and the white is Tennessee marble. On each side is a Georgian-style staircase. The National Register application notes that when Martens designed the staircases, he was inspired by architectural studies of the White House. Their newel posts are topped by finials of solid, cut crystal. Hanging from the ceiling is a restored Georgian chandelier. Also on the first floor are a ballroom, a dining room, a drawing room, a library, a sunroom and a kitchen. The chandeliers in the ballroom came from the former Scott's

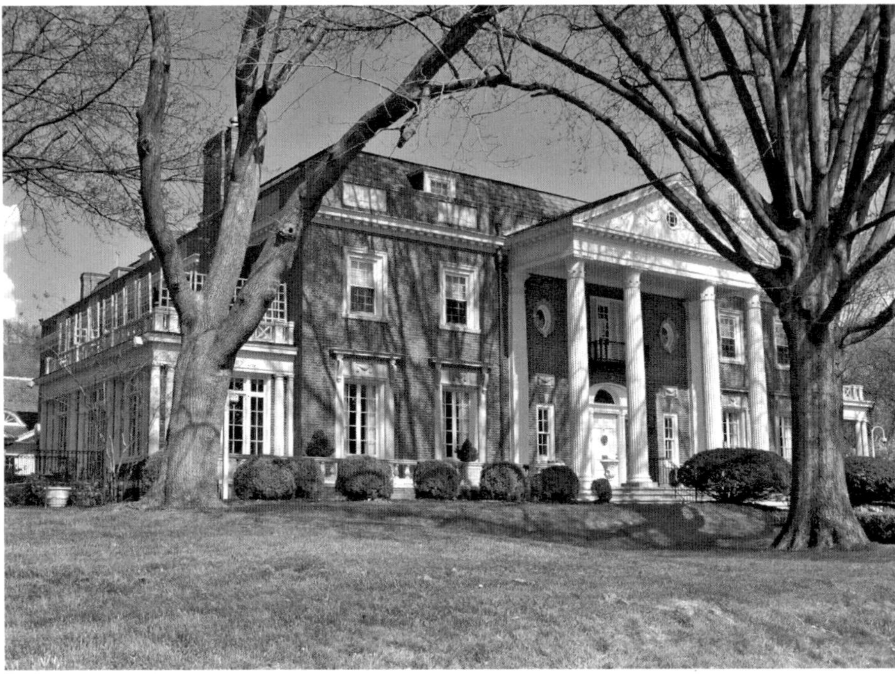

The new Governor's Mansion was built at the same time as the west wing of the Capitol, a short walk away. *Photo by Jim Wallace.*

Drug Store on Capitol Street in Charleston. Those in the drawing room once hung in the old Kanawha Hotel in Charleston. Each of those rooms also includes a notable mantel. The classic white one in the ballroom came from an Irish castle; the one in the drawing room is a replica of the mantel from the President's Cottage at The Greenbrier at White Sulphur Springs. In the dining room, a banquet table that dates back to about 1820 can accommodate twenty-two people. The library has Georgian-style butternut paneling.

The second floor contains the private quarters for the governor and the governor's family. It has eight bedrooms, four bathrooms, a small private dining room and a family room.

The first governor to occupy the mansion was Ephraim Morgan, but he did not get to enjoy it very long. His term expired in 1925, one week after he moved in.

MANY RENOVATIONS

Although Martens designed a three-story building, only two stories were built initially under a flat, tin roof. In 1946, the third floor was added, and the building was finished with two more bedrooms under an indented, mansard roof with slate shingles and dormers. Later, third-floor space was converted to exercise and entertainment rooms, but it seems to have been used for storage more than any other function.

However, the third floor was not the first addition to the mansion. A garage with servants' quarters on top was built in 1926. Also that year, an enclosed garden was added to the rear of the house.

Governors have had the mansion redecorated several times over the decades. The first significant redecoration occurred in 1937. Another occurred in 1958 during the first term of Governor Cecil Underwood. He was West Virginia's youngest governor (and forty years later, the oldest), so he and First Lady Hovah Underwood had young children. One of the changes she requested was a kitchenette near their bedroom to make it easier to prepare baby formula.

Governor Hulett Smith, who was in office from 1965 until 1969, and his wife did not get to enjoy the mansion as much as other occupants. Smith ordered an inspection of the building that revealed termite damage, dry rot, poor maintenance and fire hazards. The cost of fixing those problems and renovating the mansion came to almost $300,000. During much of the work, Smith lived in an Imperial Towers apartment nearby and his wife, Mary Alice, spent quite a bit of time at their Beckley home.

When Arch Moore returned for a third term as governor in 1985, First Lady Shelley Moore received help from Carleton Varney of Dorothy Draper & Co., an interior decoration firm based in New York City. He also was in charge of decorations at The Greenbrier. One problem the Moores ran into right away was to find furniture for the first-floor public rooms of the mansion. When the previous governor, Jay Rockefeller, and his family lived there, they brought in their own furniture not only for the private spaces but also for the public spaces. The state-owned furniture was moved next door to Holly Grove or put into storage, but it took some effort to retrieve the furniture that belonged at the mansion or find suitable substitutes.

The state funded redecoration and renovation efforts on an ad hoc basis until 1985, when Shelley Moore helped to establish the West Virginia Mansion Preservation Foundation to raise money for maintenance and furnishings. But occupants of the mansion two decades later determined that the foundation did not do enough. Gayle Manchin, who became first lady in 2005, found that the second and third floors were not maintained as well as the first floor, because the foundation's funds were used only for the part of the building open to the public. She complained about worn wallpaper and flooring, as well as carpet, which she had thrown out right away. The mansion also had leaky windows and outdated plumbing. Within a few weeks of Joe Manchin's inauguration, the couple began extensive renovations that included removing some walls and building new ones. They initially funded the work with about $500,000 left over from the money raised for the inauguration, but the bill for the renovations ran much higher.

By the middle of 2006, the Manchins could enjoy a renovated master bedroom with a sit-down steam shower and a walk-in closet. The changes also yielded three guest bedrooms on the second floor, where just two had been previously. The third floor regained two bedrooms, as well as two bathrooms, a kitchen, a sitting room and three storage areas, including one for wine and liquor. But that was not all. Much of the third floor became a combination game room, meeting room and family room with a bar and a television with a fifty-inch screen. The idea was that the room could be used not only for entertainment but also for meetings and teleconferences. Other work included having the chimneys rebuilt and the heating and cooling systems replaced. By then, what had once been estimated to be a $1.5 million project had become a $3.3 million project.

Some people objected when windows on the second and third floors were replaced by vinyl windows. Simonton Windows of Parkersburg supplied them for free, but their installation violated a Capitol Building Commission order for the mansion's original windows to be restored. However, the commission eventually accepted the new windows.

In 2007, the Manchin administration established a new, tax-exempt organization: the Executive Mansion Renovation Fund, Inc. It quickly raised several hundred thousand dollars in corporate contributions. The Manchins would have gone beyond just renovations, if they could have, with the addition of a proposed banquet hall connected to the mansion that could have accommodated 335 guests and would have had a commercial-sized kitchen. That banquet hall would have had a basement with barracks for the governor's security personnel. It would have replaced a huge $126,000 tent that stood just west of the mansion during most of the Manchin administration for use in entertaining guests at holiday parties and other events. Many critics complained about the "party tent" and the access door from the sunroom that was built without permission from the Capitol Building Commission. The tent came down early in 2011, within months after Manchin resigned as governor to take a seat in the U.S. Senate and Senate President Earl Ray Tomblin took over as governor. Despite complaints about the tent, its access door and the vinyl windows, the Manchins contended that they left the Governor's Mansion in better shape than they had found it.

Another change proposed during the Manchin administration was a security fence for the mansion grounds. It would have been made of black wrought iron with columns of brick and concrete and Victorian-style lanterns. As with the banquet hall, the fence proposal attracted much criticism, and it was not built.

HOLLY GROVE

Of all the buildings at the Capitol Complex, only one is older than the Capitol and the Governor's Mansion—older by well more than a century. Holly Grove, a large, brick house directly west of the Governor's Mansion along Kanawha Boulevard, was built sometime around 1815 by Daniel Ruffner. He built it on the site where his parents had erected their log homestead years earlier. It was a testament to how much he had prospered in the salt industry. The house had a large lawn that extended down to a boat landing along the river. It was part of a plantation that included a log barn where the Governor's Mansion now stands, as well as a granary, a smokehouse and a blacksmith shop. The plantation occupied all of modern Charleston's East End and part of the downtown district. Holly Grove got its name because many holly trees grew on the plantation.

On the stone foundation of the mansion are walls that are eighteen inches thick of heavy brick made in England. The front has a semi-circular portico two stories high with four white Ionic columns holding up a flat roof. Above the front door but under the portico roof is a wooden balcony. On the west side and at the northeastern corner of the rear section are one-story porches supported by columns. Holly Grove has three stories in the front and two in the rear, but it was not always that way. A 1974 application to put it on the National Register of Historic Places stated that "Holly Grove was originally a square, two-storied structure with a brick dining room wing extending in the rear almost to

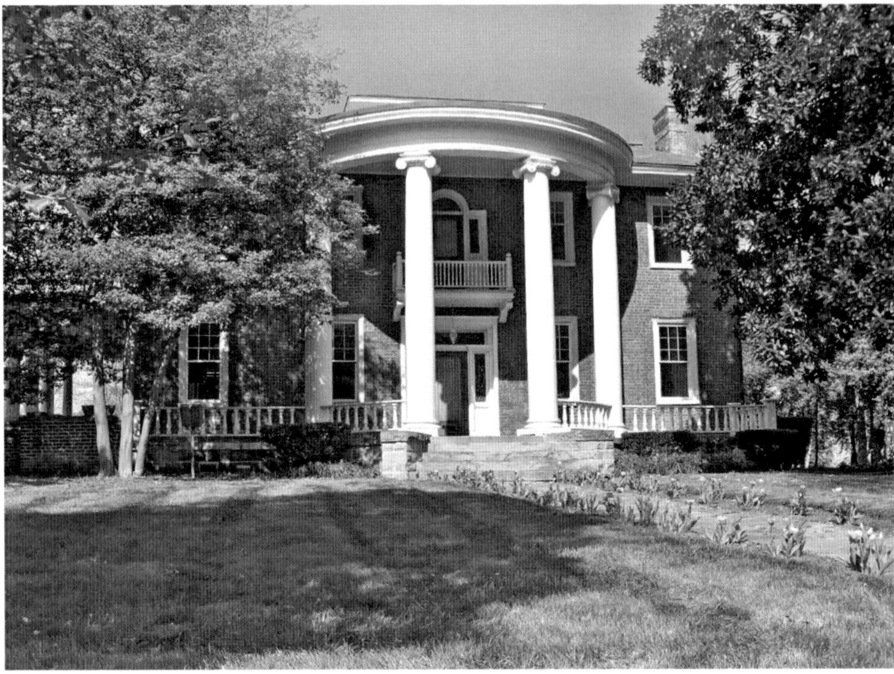

Holly Grove is now part of the Capitol Complex, but it originally was part of a huge plantation. *Photo by Jim Wallace.*

the separately housed brick kitchen. The large windows were trimmed with green shutters, and a small portico covered the front doorway which opened into a wide central hall whose rear door led to the brick-floored dining room."

The house has thirteen rooms. A fire in 1832 destroyed the original woodwork on the interior, but the walls remained, so the rooms were restored. The National Register application said each side of the hallway had square rooms with high ceilings. It also stated that the front section had wide hallways on all floors in the front section, "but the second-floor area has been shortened by a partition placed to form a room behind the balcony entrance." The application noted that a new owner who acquired the property in 1902 made many alterations including "a clever partition involving no noticeable exterior changes or interior disfigurement" so the house could be made suitable for two families.

But other changes made by the new owner, James H. Nash, contributed to Holly Grove's current appearance, as the application noted:

> *At this time the roof was raised and the former attic converted into a usable apartment. Other changes included the removal of the long dining room wing and the substitution of an indoor kitchen for the separate kitchen building. The small front portico was replaced by the present semi-circular entrance porch with its massive white columns. The red brick walls were painted gray, and the structure took a revived grace among the gardens, holly trees and boxwoods which adorned the property.*

The original owner of Holly Grove, Daniel Ruffner, was the fifth son of Joseph Ruffner, who had bought the land and moved from the Shenandoah Valley in Virginia to the Kanawha Valley in 1796. The family did well in the salt industry, which allowed Daniel Ruffner to build Holly Grove. The James River and Kanawha Turnpike ran right by it and connected Charleston to Richmond, so Ruffner advertised Holly Grove as an inn. One ad in 1826 read:

> *The subscriber has opened a house of private entertainment at his commodious residence, situate[d] one mile and a half from the town of Charleston on the road leading thence to Lewisburg. Every effort will be made to render the lodging of the traveller comfortable, and his diet palatable. His pastures are extensive and corn abundant. He will therefore be amply prepared to accomodate* [sic] *the cattle or hog merchant. For travellers on horseback, or in carriages, he will be able to furnish good stables well supplied with all kinds of provender for horses.*

Prominent people who reportedly stayed at Holly Grove included Henry Clay, Samuel Houston and John J. Audubon, as well as President Andrew Jackson, who was there in October 1832. The mansion remained in the Ruffner family's hands through the 1860s, but then ownership changed several times until Nash bought it and made his renovations.

The house was overdue for another renovation by the time it went into the National Register in 1974. The state bought Holly Grove close to that time for $140,000 when Arch Moore was governor, but it was during the administration of Jay Rockefeller, specifically under the direction of First Lady Sharon Rockefeller, that the mansion received an extensive renovation. The Rockefellers moved some Governor's Mansion furniture into Holly Grove while they used their own furniture in the Governor's Mansion.

In 1979, the West Virginia Commission on Aging moved into Holly Grove. In 1997, the Commission on Aging became the Bureau of Senior Services, and the house needed to be refurbished again. But in 2004, the bureau moved out, and Holly Grove remained vacant. Since then, state officials have had trouble figuring out what to do with Holly Grove.

In 1994, the Caperton administration proposed restoring Holly Grove and having it house nineteenth-century furniture on the first floor and office space on the upper floors. But as with other plans at the time to build a new visitors' center near the Culture Center and an amphitheater between the Culture Center and the Capitol, it never was implemented.

Rob Ferguson, secretary of the Department of Administration from 2005 until 2012, said, "If we had a lieutenant governor, it would be a good place to put him." He said the house received a new roof and many other structural repairs, although the interior was left undone pending a decision on what to do with Holly Grove. Turning it into office space would be a mistake, Ferguson said, but it might work well as a conference center with meeting rooms or a bed-and-breakfast for visiting dignitaries. "It really needs to be brought back as a house," he said. "Making that into some office space is just a bad idea."

CHAPTER 7

OTHER BUILDINGS

The new Capitol offered state government 535,000 square feet of floor space, which seemed to be plenty of room in its early years. While it was under construction, many people around West Virginia, including some newspaper writers, chastised state officials for building a structure that was bigger than they could imagine ever would be needed. However, government has a tendency to grow, and one building, even a large one, could not contain it for long. Within two decades of the Capitol's dedication, state officials decided to add another building to the campus.

BUILDING 3

In July 1945, as World War II was just weeks from ending, the State Office Building Commission, which the legislature created in 1939, entered into an agreement with Cass Gilbert Jr., son of the Capitol's architect, to design the new building, located just north of the Capitol. The location was described as "fronting Washington Street, between Duffy and Oney Streets, and extending from Washington Street, 160 feet, more or less, to an alley." In later years, Duffy, Oney and that portion of Washington Street, as well as McClung Street, all were eliminated as the Capitol Complex grew and was closed to automobiles.

The commission decided that the new building would house the Road Commission, the Department of Health, the Department of Public

Assistance and agencies handling workers' compensation and unemployment compensation. The seventh floor and part of the "penthouse" were scheduled to get the Health Department's hygienic laboratory, while the Road Commission's testing laboratory—which had been located at West Virginia University in Morgantown—was slated to go into the basement because of the heavy equipment it used. However, those plans changed by the time the building opened.

Throughout much of its existence, that building was known as the DMV Building because it housed the Department—later Division—of Motor Vehicles on the ground floor. In recent years, its formal designation has been Building 3. (The Capitol is Building 1.) Initially, the Road Commission occupied the second, third and part of the fourth floors. The Health Department got the rest of the fourth floor and all of the fifth floor. The sixth floor was shared by the Conservation Commission, the Department of Labor, the state Fire Marshal and the Insurance Commission. The Department of Public Assistance moved into the seventh and eighth floors.

Gilbert used what he called a "modified classic" design, because it maintained the classic proportions of the Capitol but ornaments and moldings were greatly simplified or eliminated. The Legislature authorized the commission to issue $2 million in revenue bonds to pay for the building, but it ended up costing $4.3 million. The construction of the building, which has eight floors with 162,075 square feet of space, did not begin right away. It was finished in 1950 and occupied in 1951. The marble lobby on the first floor contained DMV customer service windows that were used until 1998, when DMV customer service functions were moved to the Kanawha Mall. More than a decade later, other DMV offices moved to the mall.

In 1988, the Capitol Building Commission approved a plan to spend more than $1 million to build a new DMV building with on-site parking and drive-through service lanes and then move the Insurance Commission into Building 3. Part of the plan included rerouting Washington Street between Greenbrier and California Streets with a bypass going around the campus by way of Piedmont Road instead of through it between Building 3 and the Capitol. One reason cited for closing Washington Street on campus was to make room for the Veterans Memorial. Another was for the safety of pedestrians who frequently had to cross the street to go between the Capitol and Buildings 3, 5, 6 and 7. The bypass was opened that December, but the proposed building was not constructed.

By 2007, Building 3 had become worn out. "It's a beautiful building on the outside," Rob Ferguson, who was secretary of the Department of

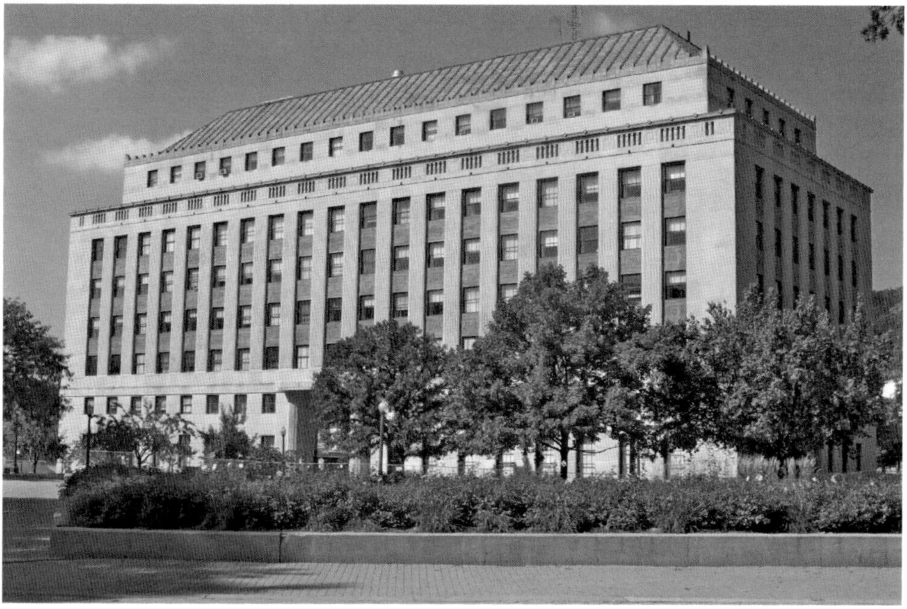

Building 3 was the first office building to be added to the campus after the construction of the Capitol. Cass Gilbert Jr., son of the Capitol's architect, designed it. *Photo by Jim Wallace.*

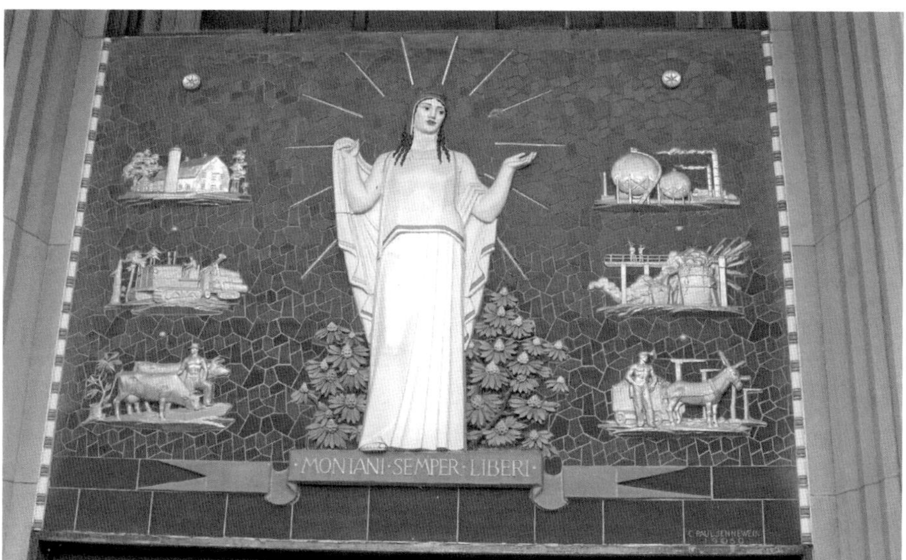

The Spirit of West Virginia is a ceramic plaque created by Paul Jennewein above the entrance on the south side of Building 3. It depicts a spirit representing the state surrounded by symbols of the state's natural resources and industry. *Photo by Jim Wallace.*

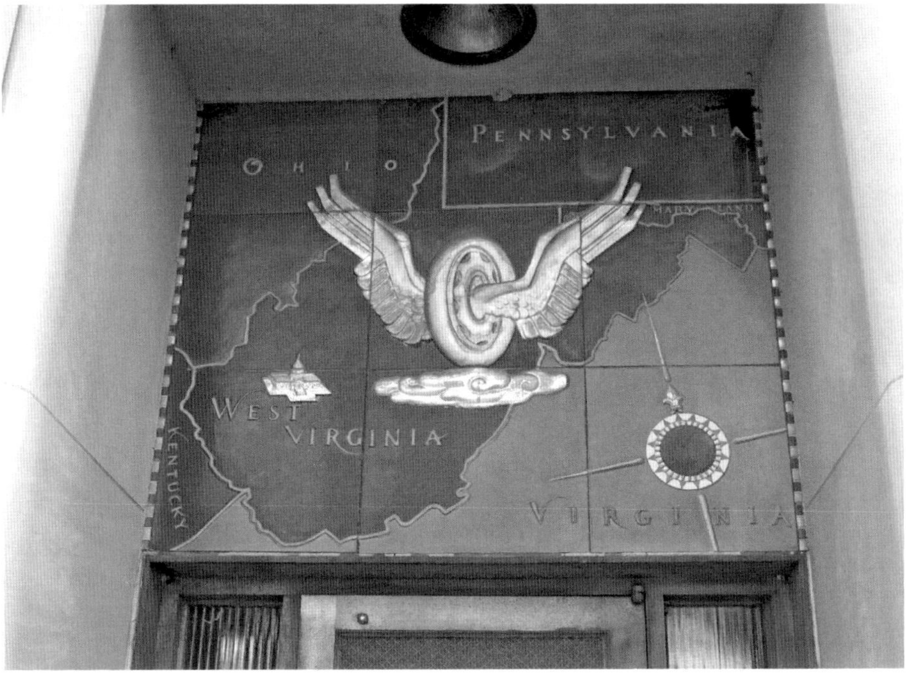

The entrance on the east side of Building 3 is topped by another ceramic plaque created by Paul Jennewein. It depicts the winged tire symbol of the Division of Motor Vehicles. Although other agencies also had offices in the building, it was known to many people as the DMV Building, because the agency had its customer service windows on the ground floor. *Photo by Jim Wallace.*

Administration from 2005 until 2012, said. "The functions were just old. It's just an old building, and it really had gotten to its service life, the mechanical systems and all systems."

State officials made plans to renovate the entire building. The project became delayed, partly by the task of relocating offices for more than seven hundred workers, but by the end of December 2010, the building was vacated. The General Services Division retained the Pittsburgh architectural firm of Perfido, Weiskopf, Wagstaff & Goettel to design the renovation. Costs for the project were estimated at $24 million and then $27 million, but when bids were opened in April 2011, the lowest was for more than $33.6 million. The plan was to preserve its historic character while updating its office space to meet twenty-first-century needs. In addition, officials wanted to make the building more energy efficient and environmentally friendly, enough so that it would be eligible for LEED (Leadership in Energy and Environmental

Design) certification. It would be the first LEED-certified building at the Capitol Complex. At the time of this writing, it was undetermined when the renovation work would be done.

GILBERT GARAGE COMES AND GOES

Cass Gilbert Jr. also designed a four-story, 216-car parking garage that was built along California Avenue in 1952 and 1953. Contractor C.H. Jimison and Sons of Charleston built the facility using reinforced concrete. It was intended to provide parking for state workers and free up spaces in a parking lot and along streets close to the Capitol for the public, but the state had trouble getting its employees to use the parking garage. Photos published in the *Charleston Gazette* in March 1954 showed many spaces in the garage were empty while nearby spaces designated for the general public were filled. In later years, many state-owned vehicles were assigned to be parked in the garage.

In 2003, the Wise administration demolished the garage, which had been designated as Building 2, because it had deteriorated to the extent that pieces of concrete had fallen from its ceilings. "I'm the one who made the decision," Tom Susman, who was acting secretary of administration at that time, later said. "We had engineering [reports] that it would cost more to fix than to tear down and rebuild it. I knew I was going to tear down the other building behind it that was an old warehouse that we were using for the Board of Risk and Insurance Management and Regional Jail Authority. That building was rat-infested. I knew if I tore it down, I would have enough parking." He said he also called a local history expert to ask if the building had any historical significance and was told that it didn't and that it was "the ugliest structure on the grounds." Susman said the fact that Cass Gilbert Jr. designed the parking garage was not enough to save it.

"The father who designed the Capitol was a well-respected architect," he said. "The son did not have the cred that the dad had, and his stuff is not nearly as revered as the dad's. And it was a public safety issue; chunks of concrete were falling."

BUILDING 4

Building 4 provides six stories of office space at 112 California Street at the corner of Washington Street, across from the east wing of the Capitol. Planning for it began in 1950, but a steel shortage and other problems delayed construction by more than two years. The building, which has 92,500 square feet of space, was completed in 1954. Newspaper reports at the time said C.E. Silling and Associates of Charleston designed the building to "express the business-type functions it will house." (However, a plaque in the building's lobby lists the architects as Tucker & Silling.) In other words, it was much plainer than the Capitol or even Building 3. The *Charleston Gazette* reported that G.W. Higginbotham of Charleston submitted the low bid of $1.541 million to become the general contractor on the project, but the delays pushed the cost up to $1.7 million. (The plaque in the building's lobby lists A.G. Higginbotham Co. as the contractor.) Winfrey Brothers, Inc., of Knoxville, Tennessee, installed the limestone facing and a base of New England marble. It was built to house offices of the Workmen's

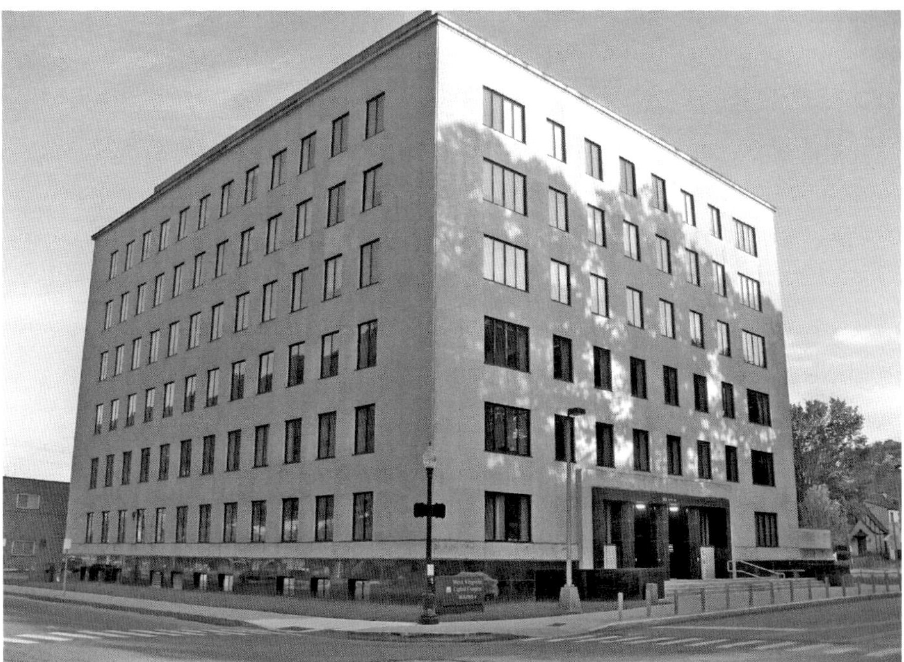

Building 4 opened in 1954, later than planned because of construction delays. *Photo by Jim Wallace.*

Compensation Commission, the Department of Employment Security and the Merit System Council. In later years, it became the home for what is now the Division of Corrections, as well as agencies that succeeded the Workmen's Compensation Commission and the Department of Employment Security, such as the current WorkForce West Virginia.

BUILDINGS THAT MIGHT HAVE BEEN

Susman, who served more than a year as secretary of the Department of Administration during the Wise administration and also served three terms in the House of Delegates, said Building 3 might have had a twin if some people had gotten their way. He said they wanted to maintain the symmetry that Cass Gilbert Sr. had provided in the Capitol's design. "There was supposed to be another building on the other side, so that the Capitol grounds would stay balanced," Susman said. "They never built that."

Published reports in 1962 indicated that state officials were upset that government agencies were paying too much for rent in privately owned buildings near the Capitol, so they were considering construction of a twin to Building 3 that would be located just north of the Capitol's east wing, just as Building 3 is located off of the west wing. A report in the *Sunday Gazette-Mail* said preliminary studies showed the building could be completed within two or three years at an estimated cost of $8 million for both the land acquisition and construction. Not only was a twin for Building 3 being considered but also so was a series of other buildings that eventually could connect the two.

"Other units in this integrated structure, developed into the master plan for the capitol more than a quarter century ago by Cass Gilbert Associates, will be built as needed," the newspaper reported.

A map of that plan showed that the additional buildings would extend north from Building 3 and its twin and then one would connect the two new ones much like the main unit of the Capitol connected its east and west wings. The result would have been a U-shaped structure with the "U" oriented in the opposite direction from the U-shape of the main Capitol. The serifs on the "U" would have been Building 3 and its twin. Together, the proposed buildings and the Capitol could have formed a large courtyard on opposite sides of Washington Street, which would still bisect the campus. The Liberty Bell, which now sits near the Capitol Circle, would have been placed at the center of the courtyard of the new set of buildings just as the Capitol Circle fountain is at the center of the courtyard between the Capitol's two wings. If that plan had been implemented, the Capitol Complex would have looked much different than it does today.

Other Plans

But instead of following that plan, state officials in the mid-1960s began making plans for another office building. Plans drawn up by the architectural firm of Zando, Martin and Milstead in 1964 called for an eleven-story building with 264,000 square feet of floor space at a cost of $7.3 million. The eleventh floor would be dedicated to air conditioning and heating equipment, so only the lower ten floors would provide office space. The architects also proposed building two five-hundred-car parking buildings and acquiring several pieces of land north of Washington Street, which still ran between Building 3 and the Capitol, so that the state would own all of the land between Duffy Street (then the western boundary of the campus) and California Street and from the Kanawha River to the south to the railroad tracks to the north.

By 1966, the State Office Building Commission had developed a new master plan that called for acquiring more land, including some west of Greenbrier Street and east of California Avenue. But another architect, C.E. Silling, denounced that as "unmitigated scatteration and civic desecration," according to the *Sunday Gazette-Mail.* He suggested that only half as much land would be needed and that Duffy Street and California Avenue should be widened to four-lane, landscaped boulevards and connected with a road that would run parallel to the railroad tracks. Silling would have left Washington Street running through the campus but lowered it by one story below ground. Also, he proposed construction of a four-story complex with two floors above ground and two below ground to serve as a receiving and distribution warehouse and public parking facility for up to two thousand cars. Further, he suggested the erection of one or more high-rise office buildings that all would be connected to Building 3. Silling received some attention in the press, but the state declined to accept his proposals.

For a twenty-first century observer, it might be hard to imagine how small the Capitol grounds were in the 1960s. Although fifty houses had been removed in the 1920s to make way for the Capitol, many houses and businesses remained close to the Capitol four decades later. Where there now is a pedestrian walkway between the west wing and the Culture Center, Duffy Street still existed then with privately owned buildings right across the street from the Capitol's west wing. Likewise, many residences still stood to the north of Washington Street, essentially in the neighborhood of the DMV Building.

"PRETTY DULL" BUILDINGS

That began to change in 1967, when the State Building Commission, which had Governor Hulett Smith as its chairman, initiated the acquisition of seventy-nine parcels to make way for not just one high-rise office building but two high-rises and a smaller building that would connect them. In addition, the state also began acquiring land between Duffy and Greenbrier Streets for use as parking lots. Revenue from parking meters was to be used to help retire bonds sold to finance the construction of the new buildings. Acquisition of that land was the beginning of the dissolution of what was known as the Rose City block along Washington Street between Duffy and Greenbrier. People who owned businesses and residences in that block fought court battles for several years in an ultimately unsuccessful effort to retain their properties.

On May 1, 1968, Governor Smith used a $41 chrome-plated shovel to lead a groundbreaking ceremony to initiate construction financed by $24.2 million in bonds for the new high-rises and related development. "Let history record that today ground is being broken not only for new structures to serve our people, but also we are breaking ground for a new era in government service," Smith said. The George A. Fuller Company, which built the west wing and main unit of the Capitol, won the $15.9 million contract to construct the new buildings. They eventually cost $16.5 million.

The new buildings provided the Capitol Complex with almost twice as much office space as Building 3 and 4 provided together. Building 5 added 247,115 square feet of office floor space over ten floors. It is a rectangular building with its long sides extending east and west. Building 6 looks similar but provides only 202,185 square feet of space over eight floors, and its long sides run north and south. They were built with precast concrete held up by 5,500 tons of structural steel. Vertical sections of Indiana limestone with small portions of granite and marble provide minimal complement to the structure of the Capitol.

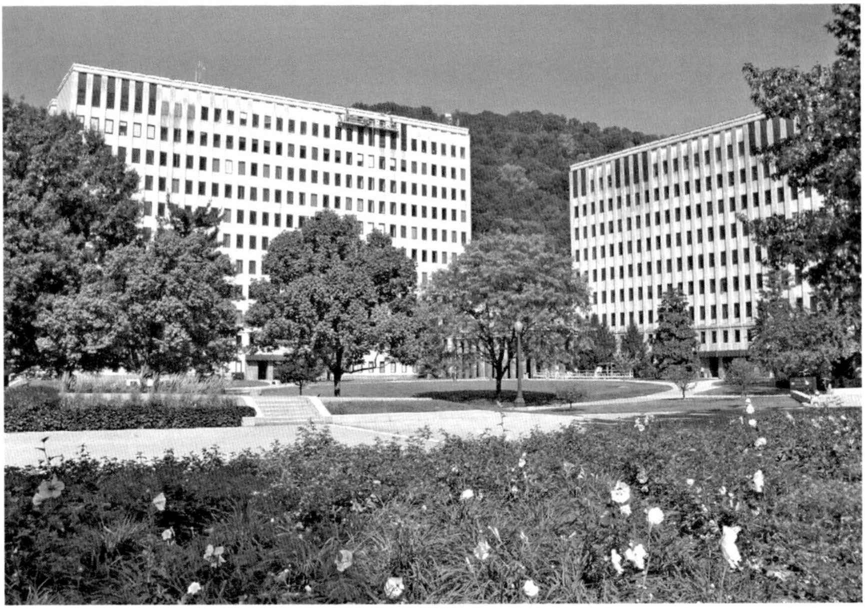

Buildings 5 (left) and 6 added much-needed office space at the Capitol Complex but have been the subject of much criticism ever since they were built. Building 7 is the two-story building between them, hidden by trees. *Photo by Jim Wallace.*

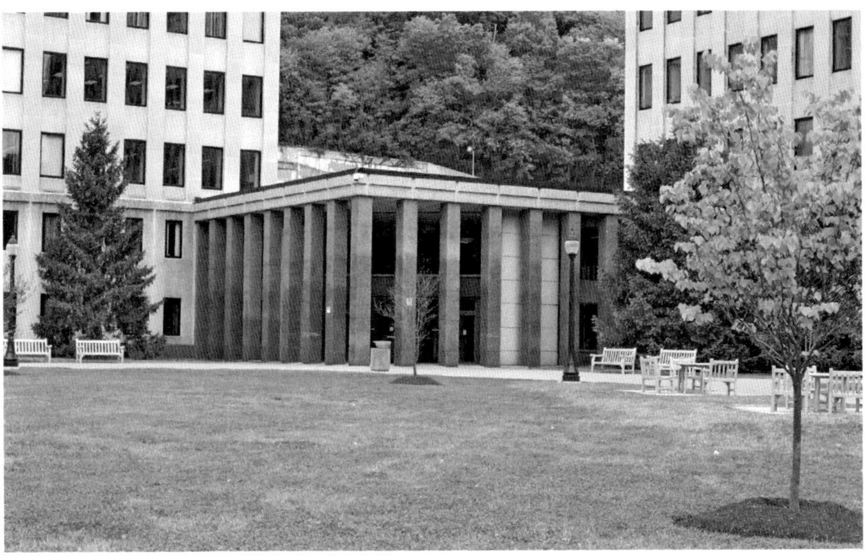

Building 7 is now called the Caperton Conference Center, but one of its main functions when it was built was to house vending machines with food for people at the Capitol Complex. *Photo by Jim Wallace.*

Building 7 is a two-story structure with 37,500 square feet of space that sits between Buildings 5 and 6 and is connected to both. Initially, its main function was to provide a large room filled with vending machines offering food to workers and visitors at the Capitol Complex, but it also had rooms for conferences.

Despite the enthusiasm Governor Smith and others expressed for adding the new buildings, they soon became the targets of criticism by many people who found the structures unsuitable companions for the Capitol. In 1971, after strike-delayed construction of the buildings was completed, a *Daily Mail* reporter found them more functional than attractive and used such words as "pretty dull" and "monotony" to describe them. Months earlier, in December 1970, Norman Fagan, who was leaving the state after serving as the executive director of the West Virginia Arts and Humanities Council (although he would return a few years later and serve fifteen years as first commissioner of the Department—later Division—of Culture and History), sharply criticized the buildings. He considered the Capitol one of the country's finest examples of Renaissance architecture but said it was desecrated by the new buildings' "Holiday Inn modern" style of architecture.

"I will say that the new buildings across from the main unit have eliminated any kind of pigeon problem because whatever the pigeons do to them, it's bound to be an improvement," Fagan told the *Gazette*. Four decades later, Rob Ferguson, shortly after he stepped down from serving as administration secretary, referred to Soviet-style architecture when he called them "the Russian buildings, because they're just terrible inside. The walls are steel, and they're movable. They're bolted together. It's just a terrible design." But he was proud of the way the administration, while he was in office, rehabilitated the tenth floor of Building 5 with an open floor space plan for the Office of Technology.

Although Building 7 was designed to serve as a conference center, it fell out of favor with many state agencies, which preferred to book more up-to-date conference and meeting rooms at hotels in downtown Charleston. That changed after Building 7 underwent about $450,000 of renovations in 2009 and 2010. The building, which by then had been given the name of the Caperton Conference Center after former Governor Gaston Caperton, acquired video-conferencing equipment, workstations with computers and high-speed Internet connections.

ADDING CULTURE

Even before Buildings 5, 6 and 7 were completed, talk had begun about putting up a building to hold archives and the State Museum. In the mid-1960s, the price for such a building was projected to be about $5 million. That talk received new impetus in 1969, when Arch Moore became governor. That April, he proposed to the Capitol Building Commission the construction of a museum and library, as well as a cafeteria, but it took until 1973 before plans were set and construction began on what was then budgeted to be a $10.6 million project.

One reason for the delay was that it required an expansion and reconfiguration of the Capitol Complex campus. Before the project started, Duffy Street still existed on the western side of the complex and Virginia Street extended to it. Duffy Street ran roughly north-south with the Governor's Mansion to the west of it and the Capitol to the east. To make way for the new building, Duffy Street had to be eliminated, and the block of Virginia Street essentially became the driveway for the Governor's Mansion. Houses and businesses in what was called the Rose City Block also had to be removed. Greenbrier Street, which then formed the western boundary of the campus, was widened.

The plan for the cafeteria was dropped, but the project went forward for a five-floor building with two floors underground and an exterior of Indiana limestone extending sixty feet high. It would have seventy-five thousand square feet of floor space with room to house about 200,000 artifacts and a 468-seat theater. The Capitol Building Commission, which was dissolved after the Capitol was dedicated in 1932, was reestablished in 1976 to monitor the construction of the Culture Center and then to maintain the architectural integrity of the entire Capitol Complex.

Construction was completed on what then was called the West Virginia Science and Culture Center by July 1976, the month the nation celebrated its bicentennial. The new center gave West Virginians even more reason to celebrate their heritage.

The celebrations began on July 6 with a black-tie affair to which Moore invited about five hundred people. Missing among them were certain key legislators, such as Senate President William Brotherton and House Finance Chairman Billy Burke. The *Charleston Gazette* suggested that they were omitted from the guest list because they had been critical of Moore and the project. Brotherton had criticized the project for going over budget with a final cost of about $14 million. Moore was known for having prickly relationships with some people, including the Democrats, who were in the majority in the

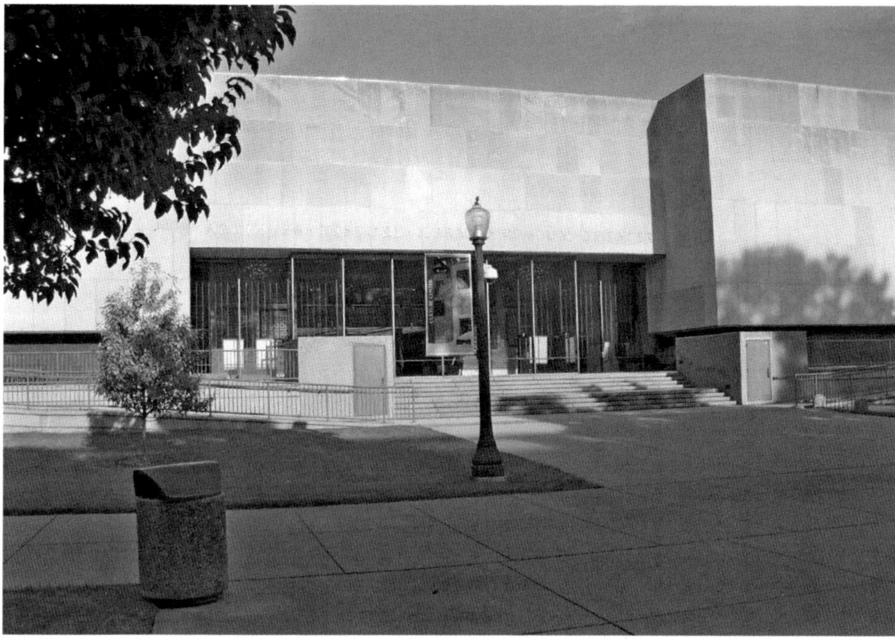

Construction of the Culture Center required the Capitol's campus to extend to Greenbrier Street and eliminate Duffy Street. *Photo by Jim Wallace.*

legislature, and news reporters. The story has been told over the years that when workers were engraving letters for "Archives" on the building, they paused after putting the first four letters up—perhaps at Moore's direction—leaving some of the governor's critics worried that he was having them put his name on the building. Some people called the center "Archie's Bunker," a reference to Archie Bunker, the lead character in the very popular television situation comedy *All in the Family*.

On July 11, thousands of West Virginians took advantage of their opportunity to see the center for the first time. Many attended free concerts by a variety of performers, including the Charleston Symphony and the Wheeling Symphony. Under sunny skies with temperatures in the nineties, they enjoyed free ice cream, soft drinks and balloons.

During the dedication ceremony, Moore said he expected the center to "encourage and foster what can only be described as the spirit of West Virginia." When he concluded by saying, "I'm proud to be a West Virginian," the audience gave him a standing ovation.

Over the decades, the building has gone from being called the Science and Culture Center to the Cultural Center to the Culture Center. It also has

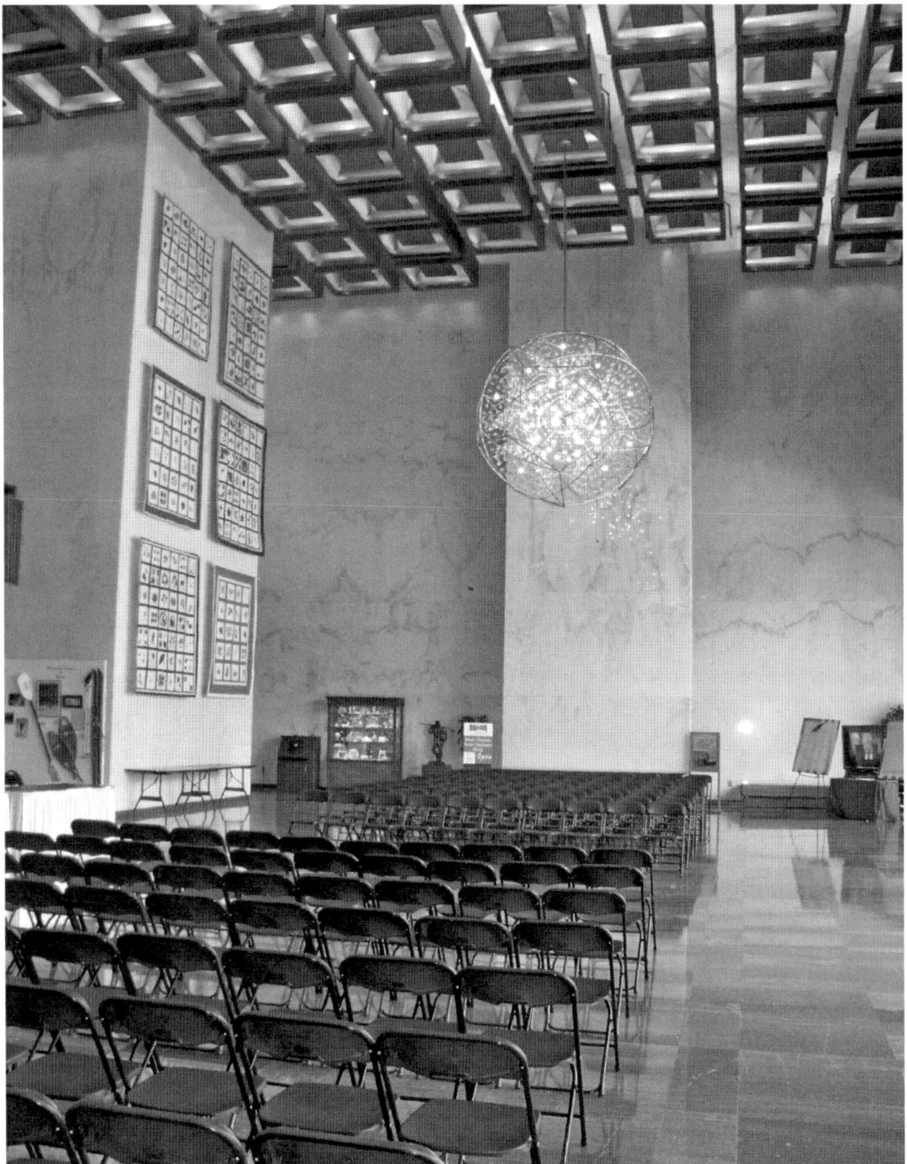

The Great Hall of the Culture Center serves as both a lobby and a performance and display space. *Photo by Jim Wallace.*

hosted a wide range of performances, workshops, exhibitions, ceremonies and receptions. In 1983, the center became the home of "Mountain Stage," a music performance show produced by West Virginia Public Radio. By June 1986, other public radio stations across the country began broadcasting the program, first through National Public Radio, then Public Radio International and then back on NPR.

STATE MUSEUM

As planned, the center became the home of the West Virginia State Museum, which dates back to 1890, when the West Virginia Historical and Antiquarian Society was organized in the Senate Chamber in the old Capitol in downtown Charleston. The society set up a display of its collection of artifacts on the first floor of the Capitol.

Within a few years, some artifacts that had been exhibited at the 1893 World's Columbian Exposition in Chicago were added to those the society already had on display. On April 3, 1894, Governor William MacCorkle announced the opening of what was then called the West Virginia State Museum in the Capitol. The society's artifacts were incorporated legally into the State Museum by an act of the legislature in 1905. The museum then moved into the Capitol Annex, which had been built two years earlier. That move saved the museum's collections sixteen years later when the Capitol caught on fire.

After the new Capitol opened in 1932, the museum took up residence in the basement. But over the next four decades, the collections grew so much that the museum became cramped for space, which led to the effort to build the Culture Center. Once again, the museum was put in the basement, but in the Culture Center, it had environmental controls to help preserve the artifacts.

For the next two decades, the museum exhibited such displays as a complete log cabin, a Conestoga wagon, war souvenirs, fossils and occasionally Alexander and Emmiline, a pair of fleas donated in 1906. Alexander was dressed in a suit with black pants, while Emmiline wore a dress with a white skirt. They had to be viewed through a magnifying glass, but they were quite popular.

However, by the late 1990s, an old itch emerged that had nothing to do with fleas. It was the desire of some people for a better museum, one with exhibits that would be less static and more interesting. In 1999, the Legislature granted the administration of Cecil Underwood almost $1 million during that fiscal year and $1.5 million in the following year to initiate an extensive renovation of the museum. The plan was for lawmakers to appropriate another $1.5 million the year after that and for raising another $2 million in donations.

Consultants from Christopher Chadbourne and Associates of Boston helped the staff of the Division of Culture and History hold public meetings to come up with ideas for what the new museum should be like. They talked about having interactive displays with state-of-the-art technology. The projection was for the new museum to open in the fall of 2001, but it repeatedly fell behind schedule. One part of it that was completed was construction of a curved exhibit case on the first floor of the center meant to be an introduction to the museum and entice visitors downstairs to see seven other galleries. Preliminary names for some of those galleries were: "The Land and the People," "Frontier Heritage," "Becoming a State," "Defending the Nation," "Connecting West Virginia" and "West Virginia Works." The latter was to be the largest, covering about five thousand square feet on the north side of the building with exhibits devoted to industry, including one showing the evolution of coal-mining processes.

In 2001, Bob Wise succeeded Underwood as governor. Initially, the new administration just put off further work on the museum while newly appointed officials examined the renovation plans. Then they had the introductory exhibit case dismantled. Among the problems they had with the plans was that the museum would have portrayed the state's history only up until 1900, and they wanted to include the twentieth century.

In 2002, a report from the Legislative Auditor's Office harshly criticized the storage of archives and artifacts. The report said, "There is inadequate protection and risk of loss to the archives and museum collections because of improper storage and insufficient fire protection." The storage and work areas were "extremely cluttered and appeared disorganized."

In January 2004, the State Museum, which was still in its old setup, shut down for a renovation that was expected to take ten months. The Wise administration had contracted with Matthew Martin Designworks, a company based in California with experience developing theme parks for Disney and Universal Studios. The new museum was supposed to not only have interactive displays but also cover the full range of West Virginia's history and prehistory. The project bogged down again that fall when the Division of Culture and History realized it would cost more than the $7.45 million then budgeted for it.

In January 2005, the Legislative Auditor's Office again issued a critical report. This time it was for the project's spending of almost $1 million for work by Matthew Martin Designworks and about $850,000 on escalators without getting the legislature's permission. Shortly after that report was issued, Joe Manchin became governor, so responsibility for the project passed on to a new administration.

In November 2007, the state awarded a contract of almost $4 million to the Maynard C. Smith Company of Charleston to do the general contracting work on the project. In June 2008, Design and Production, Inc., of Lorton, Virginia, received a contract for the specialty work of creating and installing the museum's exhibits. The Manchin administration also contracted with consultant James Scott Hunt of Charlotte, North Carolina, to oversee the renovations. The newly designed museum was to display about twelve thousand of the fifty-eight thousand artifacts in the agency's collection.

After a decade of delays, false starts and budget busting, the new museum with twenty-four thousand square feet of exhibits opened to the public on West Virginia Day, June 20, 2009. The cost in the end was $17.3 million, almost three times the original projection.

As visitors descend from the first floor of the Culture Center, the recorded voice of the governor greets them. When they leave the State Museum, a similar recording thanks them for coming.

The museum has a central, 660-foot-long show path that goes from prehistoric West Virginia to the present. As visitors walk along it, the floor changes its appearance to reflect the time of the exhibits from dirt paths to cobblestone streets to asphalt roads. Date plates in the floor indicate where along the timeline visitors have reached. Along the way, they have the opportunity to explore twenty-six discovery rooms with information about specific periods and events: An Ancient Land, Prehistoric People, Conflict and Settlement, Frontier Life, John Brown's Raid, The War within a State, The Case for Statehood, The Big City, The Family Farm, The Company Store, Changing Roles of Women, Trains and Railroads, Boats and Rivers, Industrialization (with exhibits for oil and gas; glass, pottery, steel and metalworking; chemical and timber; and industrial film), The Mining Life, The State Capitol, It's Not All Work, The Great Depression, The Mine Wars, West Virginians at War, Late Twentieth Century, Celebrating West Virginia, From Here to There, Painting and Sculpture, A Legacy of Craftsmanship and Traditions of Music. It has been estimated that it would take about twenty-six hours for someone to take in all of the museum's offerings, including documentary videos and audio recordings.

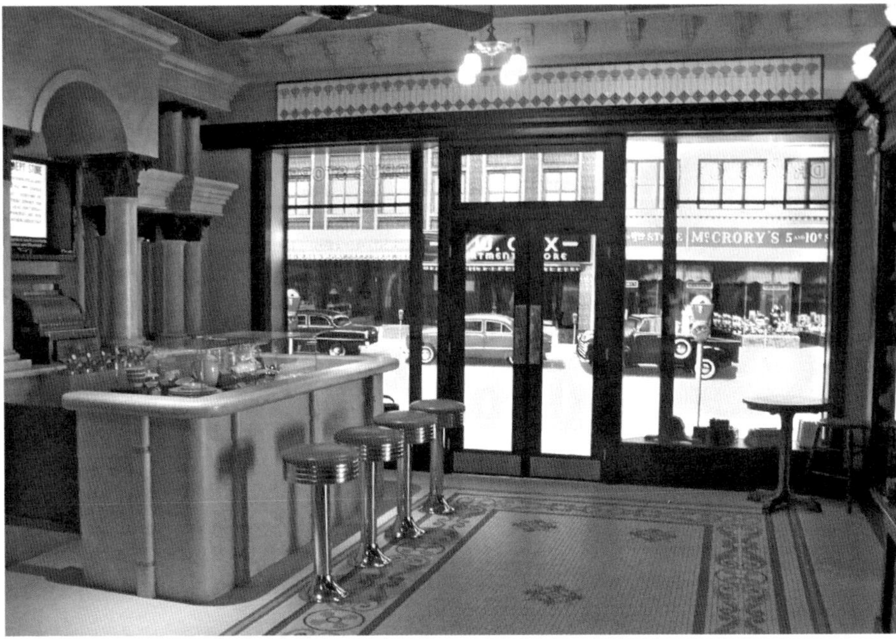

The State Museum has changed its look and location many times. The last renovation took several years before the museum reopened to visitors in 2009. Among the exhibits is this reproduction of the interior of the former Scott Brothers Drug Store in downtown Charleston with a soda fountain and a view of Capitol Street as it looked in the 1950s. *Photo by Jim Wallace.*

In July 2009, shortly after the State Museum opened, the building that houses it took back the name Culture Center after years of being known as the Cultural Center. It was a minor change but one that officials at the Division of Culture and History thought needed to be made for grammatical and promotional reasons.

Along with the State Museum, the center houses the State Archives Library, the State Historic Preservation Office, other Division of Culture and History offices, a theater and a gift shop.

New Garage

Parking often has been a problem around the Capitol. When legislators, lobbyists and other visitors are added to the thousands of people who work at the complex on a daily basis, it can be hard to find room for all of their vehicles. Because of that problem, legislators decided to provide funding for a four-level, 764-space parking garage, designated Building 13, which was built in 1999 in the northwestern corner of the campus near Greenbrier Street and Piedmont Road at a cost of $5.6 million. But seven years later, it suffered from cracked concrete, rusted pipes, water leaks and other problems that were blamed on a lack of maintenance. An engineering firm estimated it needed $3.1 million in repairs. Those repairs were added to the long list of fixes that needed to be made around the complex.

Years later, Rob Ferguson, the administration secretary who had to see that the repairs were made, said the garage never should have been built. "You can't find an architect anywhere or an engineer anywhere that will tell you today that it was a good idea," he said. "It's just a terrible place to put it. It's a waste of real estate."

BEYOND CAMPUS

In addition to Building 4, the state owns a few other buildings east of California Avenue. They are part of the Capitol Complex, but there are still private houses around them, so the eastern edge of the campus is not defined as clearly as the western, northern and southern edges are. Also, contrary to the situation for many years after the Capitol was completed in 1932, state government offices are far from contained within the Capitol grounds. Many agencies have moved back to downtown Charleston in renovated buildings close to where the former Capitol stood, as well as elsewhere. Most notable is the Department of Health and Human Resources, which occupies the former Diamond department store building that stands precisely at the location of the Capitol that burned down in 1921. In 2011, the Lottery Commission moved into City Center West, a thirteen-story building the commission bought for its own use as well as that of other agencies.

Other agencies have built new facilities designed specifically for their needs, such as the Department of Environmental Protection's building (shared with the Public Employees Insurance Agency) and the Housing Development Fund's building, both in the Kanawha City section of Charleston. Although most agencies have their headquarters in Charleston, as the state Constitution seems to require, a few of them are located outside the city. The earliest agency to move outside Charleston seems to have been the State Police. Records show that State Police headquarters have been in South Charleston since 1938. In 2003, when Kanawha County officials went to court to prevent the Lottery Commission from moving its headquarters to Putnam County, Tax Secretary Brian Kastick said his office needed thirty-seven pages to provide a list of the location of every state government office. Not all of them were state agency headquarters, but the size of that list is an indication of how much office space it takes in the twenty-first century to house state government, which once was contained entirely within a three-story building in Wheeling that the state rented from Linsly Institute.

Chapter 8

Statues, Busts, a Bell and More

The grounds and hallways of the Capitol are a combination art gallery and history museum. That is what Cass Gilbert intended. It was Gilbert who had a dozen busts of Greco-Roman deities and heroes placed on entrances to the building, which gives some indication of the type of artwork he wanted for the rest of the Capitol grounds. He called for "artists of established reputation and experience and of real quality" to provide sculpture and mural decorations. In his letter to Governor Conley, Gilbert said the artwork at the Capitol should be of "the highest standards of good taste."

Gilbert also suggested that selection of artists and experts should be made by the architect. However, after construction of the Capitol ended in 1932, the state did not have funds to add statues and other artwork, and Gilbert died less than two years later, so he had no opportunity to design such works let alone choose the artists for them. But he did warn West Virginians that without such guidance "there will be intrusion of incidental sculpture and decorations in questionable taste."

At the time Gilbert wrote his letter to Conley, he noted that "at the present time there are two statues temporarily located on the site and another one recently installed, the disposition of which I should like to discuss with the commission." That seems to indicate that Gilbert did not approve of the two statues that had been moved over from the site of the previous Capitol and another accepted since the earlier Capitol burned down. But he did not get his way on that matter, and they became the first three statues installed on the new Capitol grounds.

Since then, similar statuary and other artwork that honor prominent West Virginians and the causes that have been important to the state throughout its history have been placed on the grounds.

CIVIL WAR STATUES

Fitting for a state born of the Civil War with residents who were divided by it, statues on the Capitol lawn honor combatants for both the Union and the Confederacy, as well as the president who led the nation through the war and a man who was born a slave and went on to become a renowned educator.

The oldest of the statues stands near the southeastern corner of the Capitol lawn. It stood originally at the northwestern corner of the grounds of the previous Capitol downtown, where it was dedicated in 1910. It depicts Thomas Jonathan Jackson, who was better known as "Stonewall" Jackson, one of the most famous Confederate generals. He was born in Clarksburg in 1824 and grew up at Jackson's Mill in Lewis County. He died in 1863 after his own troops accidentally shot him, leading to the amputation of his left arm and then pneumonia. His bronze statue is intended to honor Confederate soldiers from the part of Virginia that became West Virginia. The United Daughters of the Confederacy commissioned Moses Ezekiel, who also served as a Confederate soldier, to design the statue. Its unveiling on September 27, 1910, followed a parade of Confederate veterans down Capitol Street. The *Charleston Gazette* reported that Governor William Glasscock had given permission for the flag of the Twenty-second Virginia Infantry to be carried, but it was not carried by the veterans themselves. The statue was moved to the grounds of the new Capitol in 1926. At that time, it was near the newly completed west wing. The statue was moved to its current location in 1976, when the Culture Center was built. A replica of the statue stands at the Virginia Military Institute in Lexington, Virginia.

The *Stonewall Jackson* statue did not stand very long on the lawn of the former downtown Capitol before the Union received equivalent recognition in the form of the *Mountaineer Soldier* statue. The inscription on the west side of its base states: "Erected to commemorate the valor of those who on April 15, 1861, in instant response to the first call of Abraham Lincoln formed themselves into the intrepid Home Guards who held in check unaided the

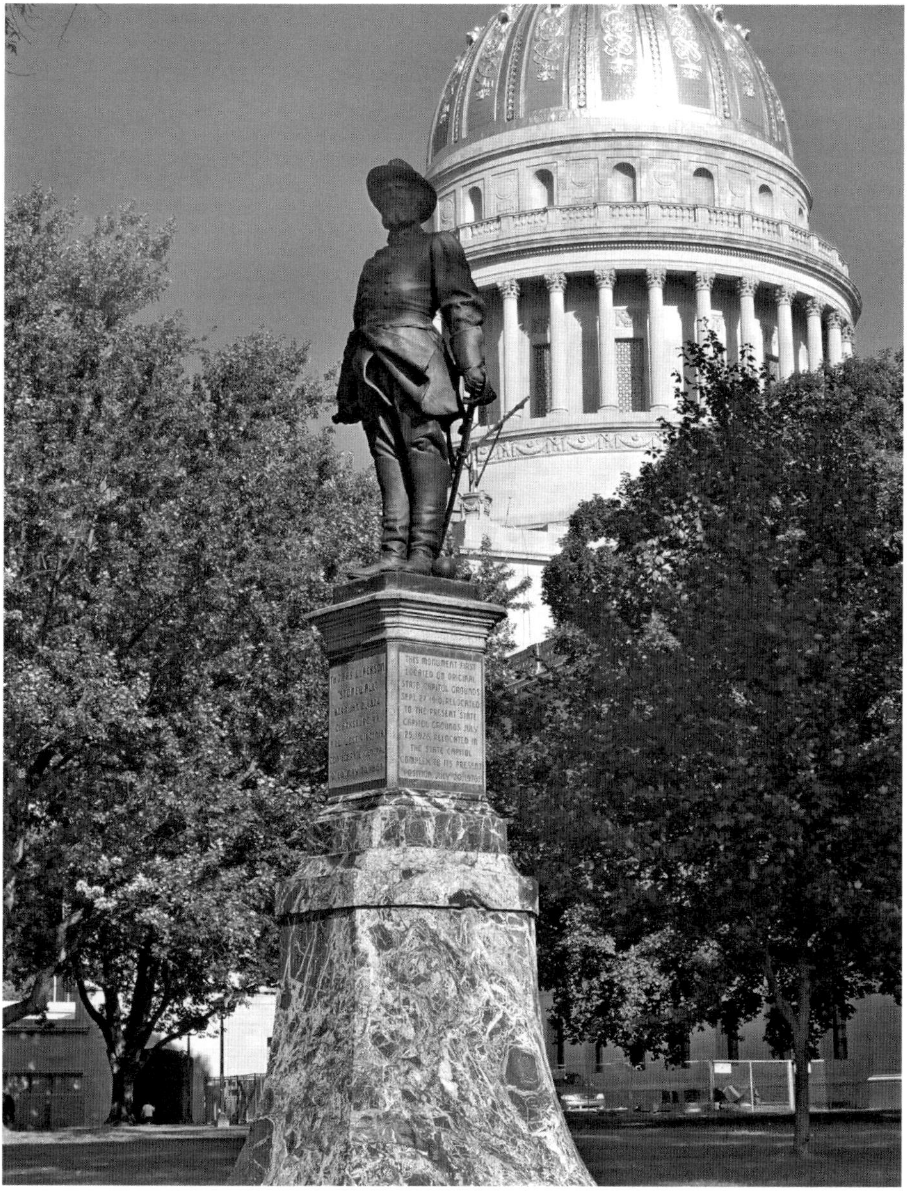

The statue of Stonewall Jackson originally stood on the grounds of the former Capitol in downtown Charleston before it was moved to the current Capitol campus. *Photo by Jim Wallace.*

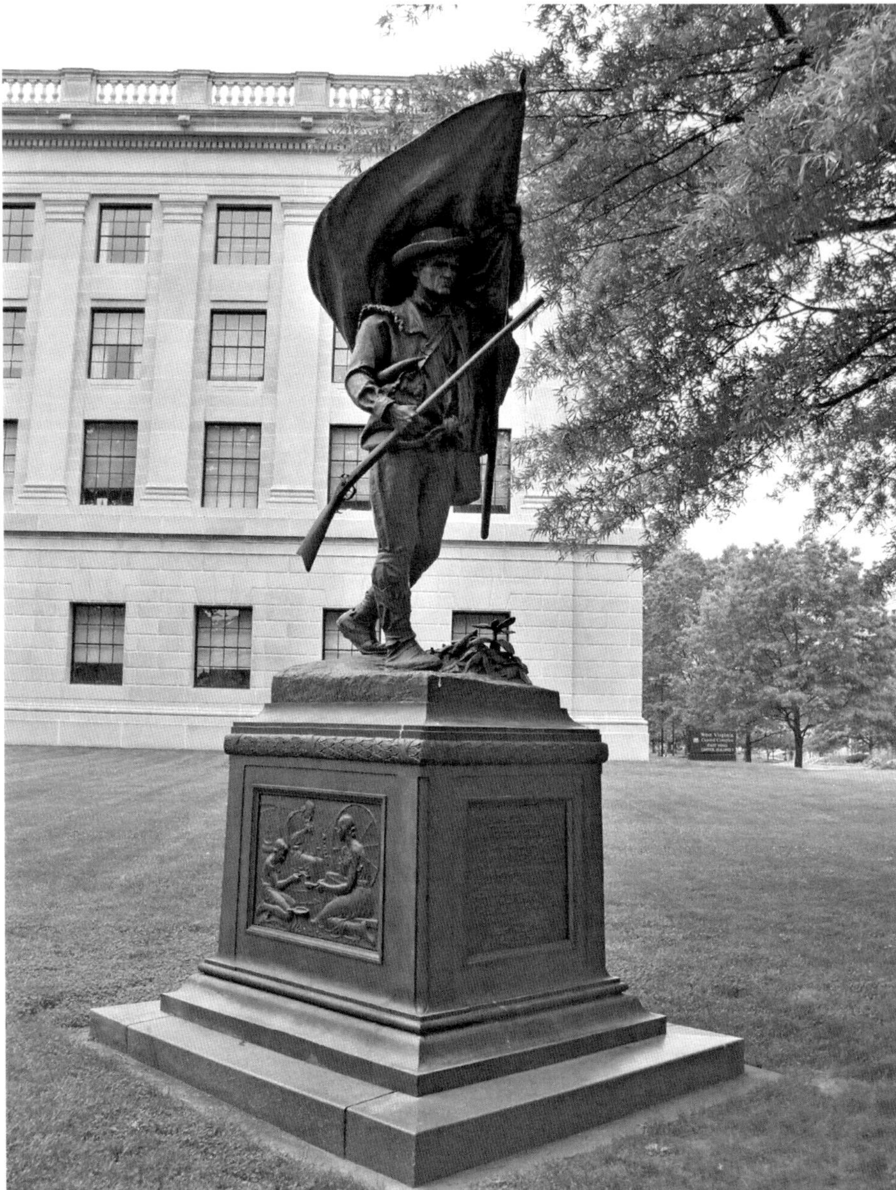

The *Mountaineer Soldier* statue soon joined Stonewall Jackson on the old Capitol's lawn, and they moved together to the new Capitol. *Photo by Jim Wallace.*

forces of Wise, and Lee, and Jackson, until the federal armies came…" The statue depicts a soldier carrying a billowing U.S. flag and a musket. Sculptor Henry K. Bush-Brown had Eli Hamrick, nicknamed "Rimfire," a six-foot-three mountaineer from Webster County, pose as his model. The statue was dedicated in 1912. It now stands near the northeastern corner of the east wing of the Capitol, within sight of the Jackson statue. Although Jackson has a prominent position on the Capitol lawn, the Mountaineer to his north and the Lincoln and the Union soldier statues to his west seem to remind him which side won the Civil War.

Near the southwestern corner of the Capitol lawn is a statue of a Union soldier with a rifle on his right shoulder, seemingly marching toward Jackson's statue. This is the *Soldiers and Sailors Monument*, which is a memorial to about thirty-two thousand West Virginians who fought for the Union during the Civil War. West Virginia's Soldiers and Sailors Memorial Commission had it erected in 1927. Rob Ferguson, who served as administration secretary from 2005 until 2012, said the Union soldier statue was one of many such statues that were produced for distribution in many states. "It's a pretty statue, but apparently it's pretty cheap," he said. "We had it taken down when the base started falling apart and had it fixed. It wasn't the highest quality statue according to Joe Mullins [sculptor of other statues at the Capitol Complex]."

Between the statues of Jackson and the Union soldier is one of President Lincoln, who signed the bill and issued the proclamation that made West Virginia the thirty-fifth state. It is named *Abraham Lincoln Walks at Midnight* and is based on the poem with the same title written by Vachel Lindsay in 1914. As the title indicates, the statue depicts Lincoln wearing a robe and pacing, apparently troubled by the strains of being a wartime president. Fred Torrey of Fairmont designed the statue in the 1930s, but he died in 1967, several years before sculptor Bernie Wiepper of Charleston was contracted to produce the nine-and-a-half-foot version that now stands facing the Kanawha River in front of the steps on the south side of the Capitol. Governor Arch Moore and other dignitaries dedicated the statue on West Virginia Day, June 20, 1974. The inscription on the west side of the statue's base states: "Funds for statue contributed by school children of West Virginia and other interested citizens."

On the opposite side of the Capitol from the Jackson, Lincoln and Union soldier statues, a bronze bust of Booker T. Washington sits facing out to the north from the end of the west wing. Washington was born into slavery in Franklin County, Virginia, in 1856. The Civil War freed his family,

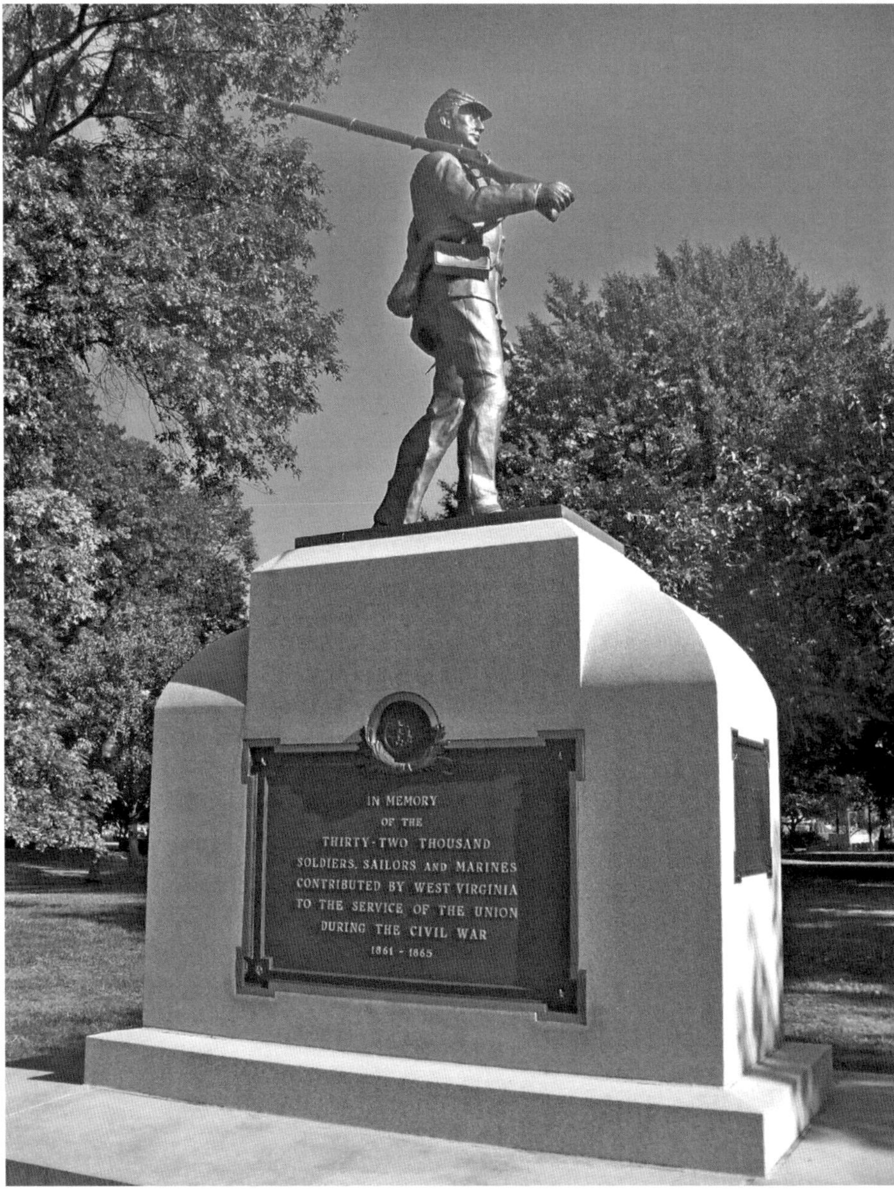

What is formally called the *Soldiers and Sailors Monument* is commonly known as the Union Soldier statue. It was erected on the grounds before the Capitol was completed. *Photo by Jim Wallace.*

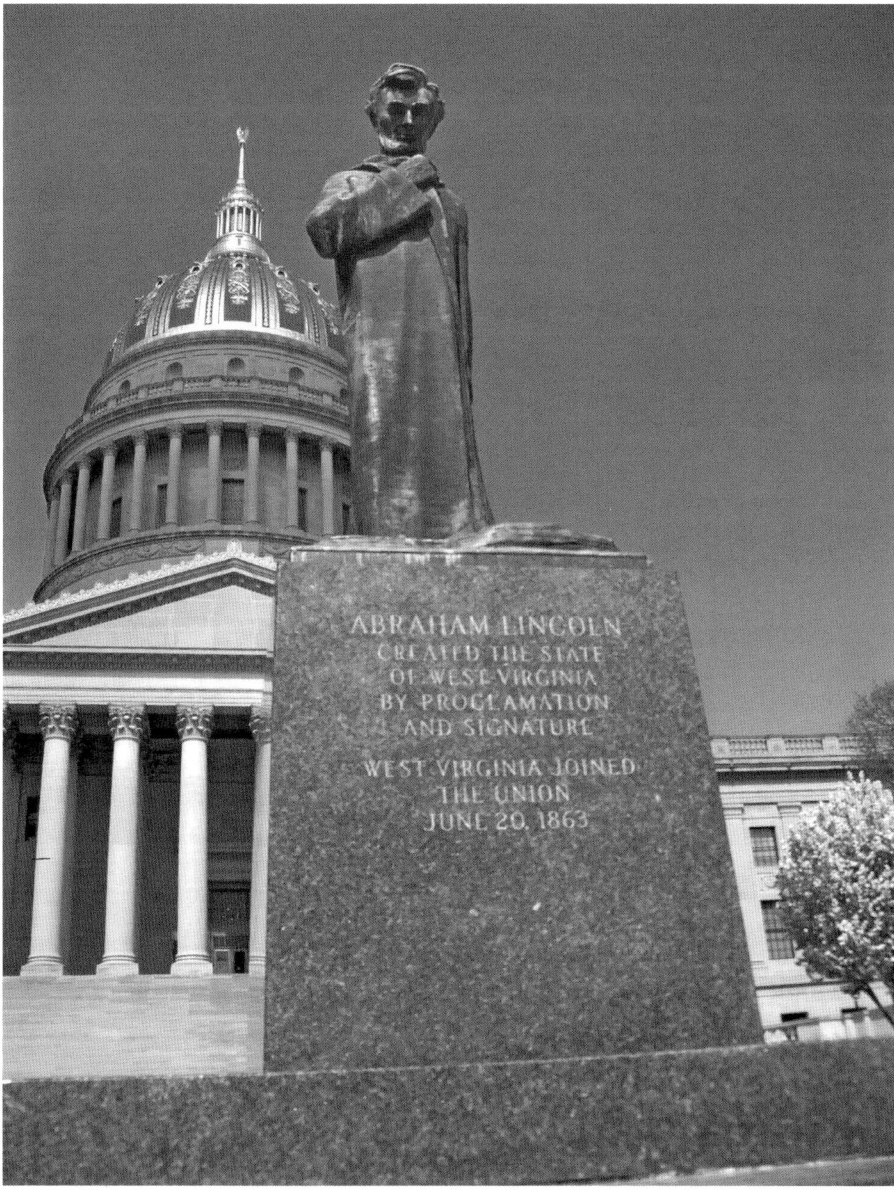

The *Abraham Lincoln Walks at Midnight* statue honors the president who signed the statehood bill for West Virginia. *Photo by Jim Wallace.*

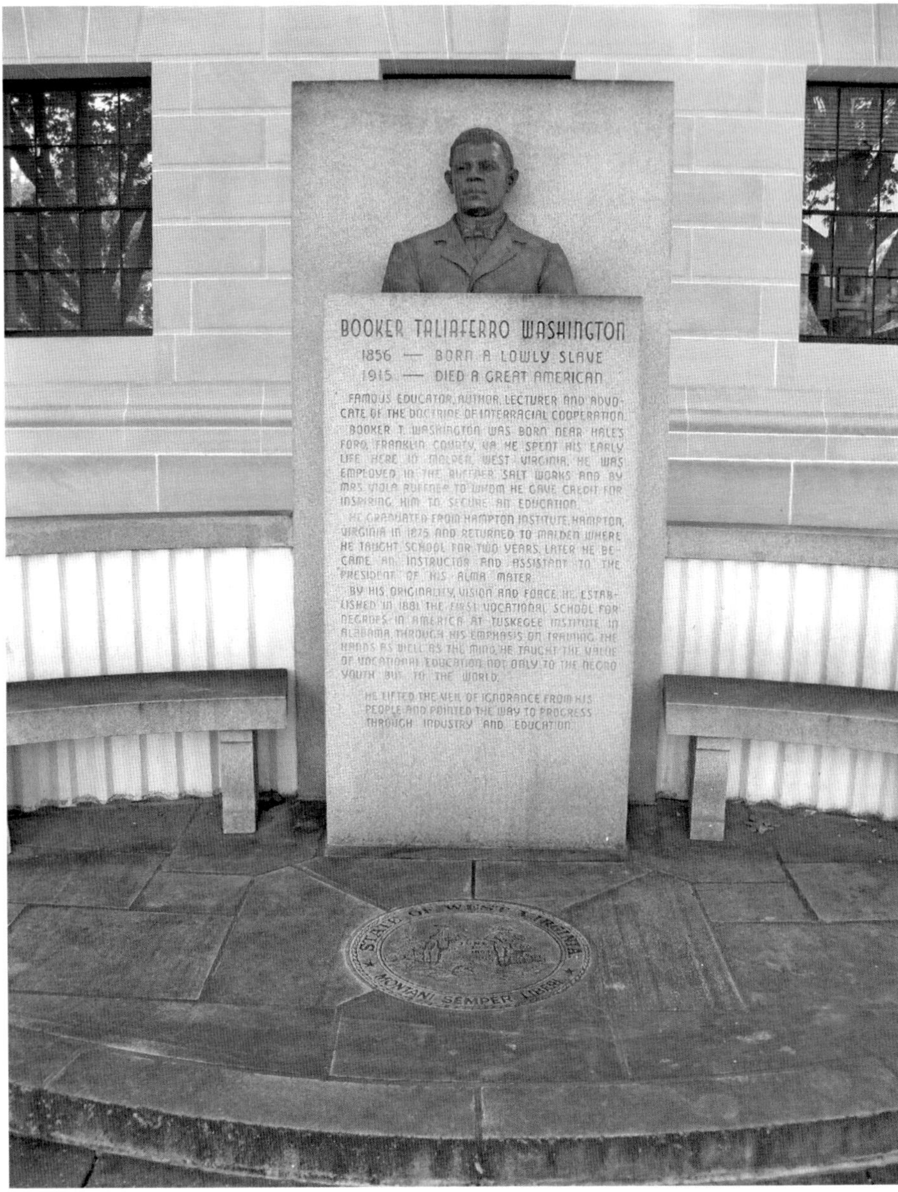

The Booker T. Washington bust at the Capitol replaced one that had been vandalized at Malden. *Photo by Jim Wallace.*

which moved to Malden near Charleston in 1865. After several years in West Virginia, Washington received an education at Hampton Institute in Virginia before returning to West Virginia to begin his career as an educator. He later established the Tuskegee Institute in Alabama. It was the first vocational school for African Americans in the country. Washington's granddaughter, Margaret Washington Clifford, joined Governor Arch Moore in unveiling the bust in 1985. It replaced another bust that had been vandalized along Route 60 at Malden before being moved to the Capitol Complex. The sculptor of the new bust, Bill Hopen of Braxton County, had hoped to create more than just a bust. He suggested a sculpture with a hand holding a book and a wrist with a manacle and a broken chain to symbolize freedom from slavery. But the Booker T. Washington Foundation, which commissioned the work, preferred to stick with a bust similar to the one it replaced.

VETERANS REMEMBERED

Obviously, the Civil War period is represented well on the Capitol grounds. Late in the twentieth century, combatants in more recent wars also received recognition. The effort to honor veterans of World War I, World War II, the War in Korea and the War in Vietnam began in the 1980s, but it took until 1999 for the West Virginia Veterans Memorial to be completed.

In 1985, a legislative resolution and an executive order from Governor Moore called for the creation of a commission to raise private donations to build a memorial to Vietnam War veterans on the Capitol grounds. But some veterans objected because they wanted a memorial for veterans of all wars, perhaps even with room to recognize those from wars that had not yet been fought. By 1987, when the commission selected a winner from thirteen finalists out of 180 entries in a competition to design the memorial, the plan was to honor veterans of the four major wars of the twentieth century.

The winner was Joseph Mullins, a Charleston resident with a master's degree in fine arts. He designed a circular structure of granite and Indiana limestone divided in four by walkways that lead into its interior with panels engraved with the names of veterans who died in each of the four wars. The outside of each section has an alcove with a sculpture representing one of

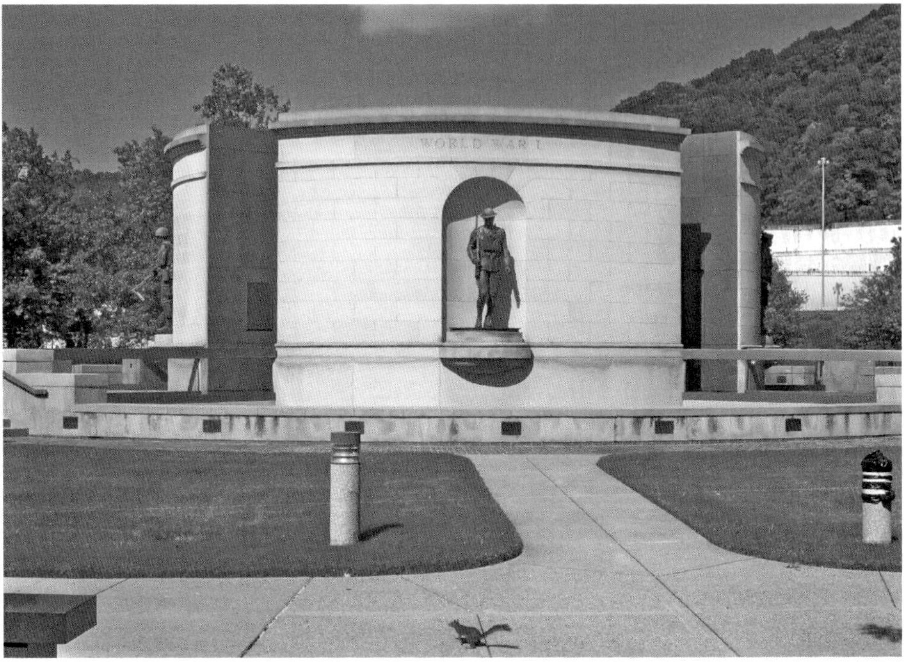

The Veterans Memorial honors West Virginians who served in the major wars of the twentieth century. *Photo by Jim Wallace.*

the wars and one of the four branches of the military under the jurisdiction of the Department of Defense: a World War I soldier, a World War II sailor, a Korean War airman and a Vietnam War marine. The memorial is surrounded by a reflecting pool.

At the time, state officials hoped the memorial would be finished by Veterans' Day in 1988, but raising funds for it proved to be more difficult than expected. However, during 1988, the state closed the block of Washington Street that went through the Capitol Complex to make room near Building 3 for the memorial. On August 14, 1989, Governor Gaston Caperton dedicated the site of the Veterans Memorial Plaza, saying, "No state has made a greater contribution to our nation's defense than West Virginia." He noted that the state accounted for just 1 percent of the country's population but 8 percent of its veterans.

The foundation for the memorial was completed in 1991, but fundraising for the rest of it still lagged. In 1994, the legislature decided to allocate a portion of video lottery revenues to the project until it was finished. Oshel Craigo, who was vice-chairman of the Senate Finance Committee, came

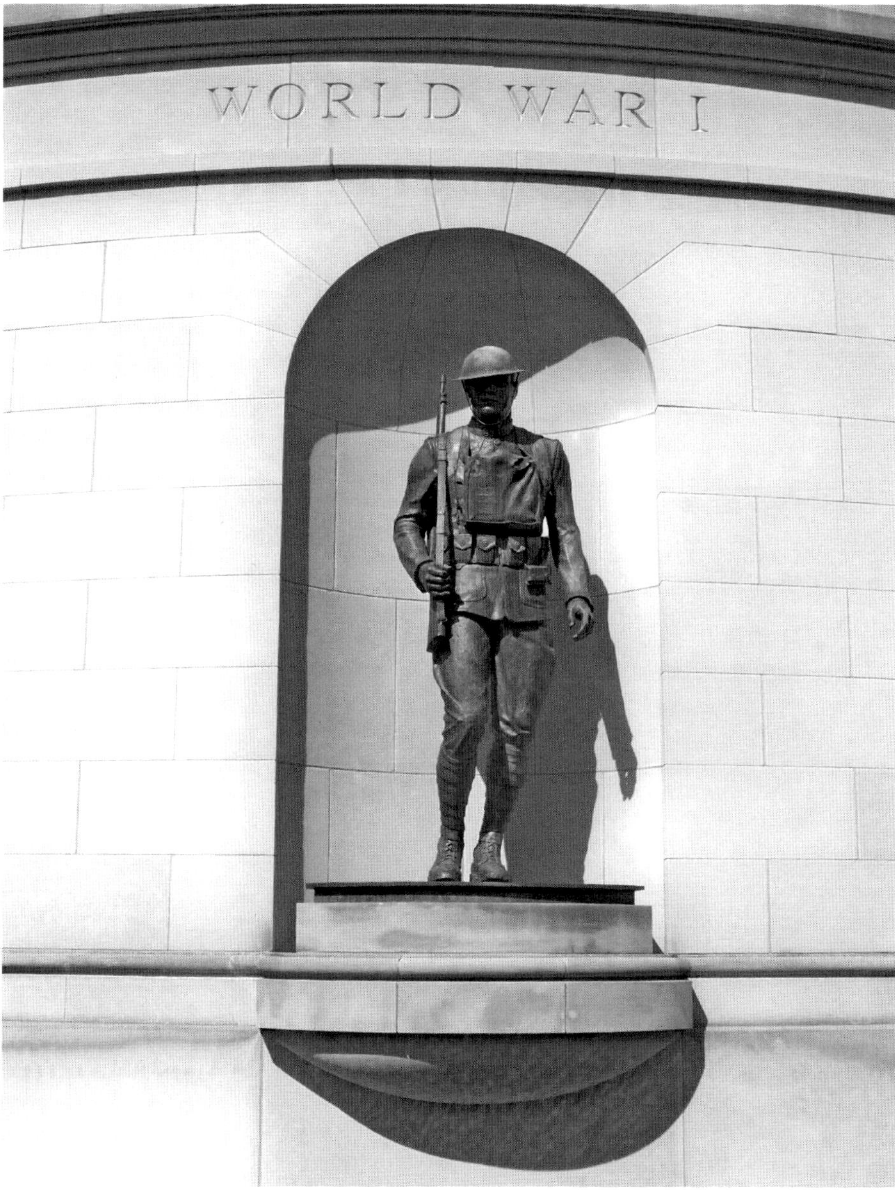

A World War I soldier statue represents U.S. Army veterans. *Photo by Jim Wallace.*

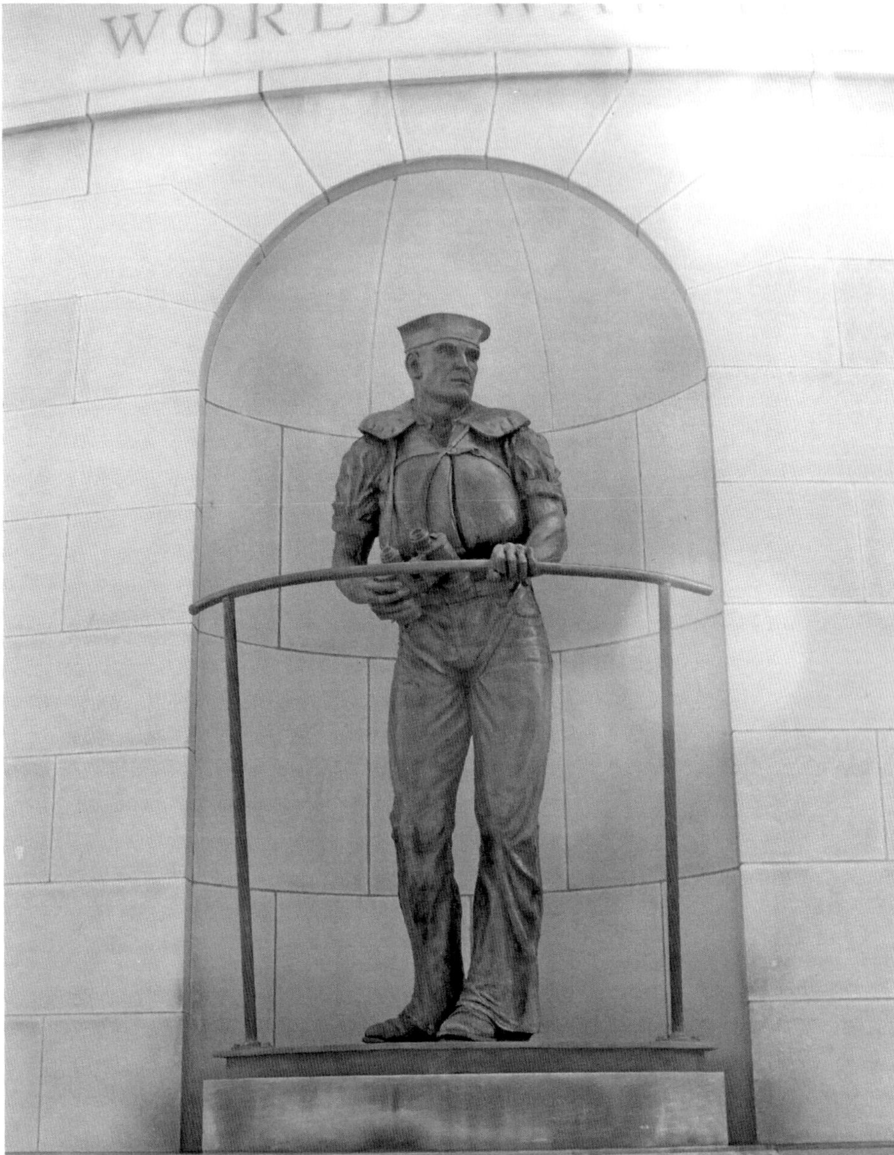

A World War II sailor statue represents U.S. Navy veterans. *Photo by Jim Wallace.*

up with that idea and got approval from Earl Ray Tomblin, who then was chairman of the committee and later would become Senate president and governor. Craigo said he decided on that course after coming out of the Capitol late one evening and seeing the unfinished memorial site. Over the next year, Craigo also helped work out a $1.3 million line of credit, which got work on the project moving swiftly. A ceremony on Veterans Day 1995 unveiled the memorial to the public, but the four sculptures had yet to be installed, partly because funding for them had not been raised yet. The final sculpture, the Vietnam War marine, was lowered into position just a day before a Veterans Day 1999 ceremony, when Governor Cecil Underwood unveiled it. The interior of the monument contains the names of more than ten thousand veterans from West Virginia who lost their lives in the four wars. The memorial cost about $3 million.

That could have been the end of the effort to honor West Virginia's veterans, but it wasn't. There were problems with the names etched into the memorial: 890 had been omitted and 146 had misspellings or other errors. The black granite panels were ground down and re-etched. That project cost about $350,000 and took about three years. It was completed in 2009, shortly before Veterans Day.

But errors with the names weren't the only problems with the memorial. Although the new monument represented all four of the major wars of the twentieth century and four branches of the military, many people complained that it left out one important category of veterans: women. In 1999, the legislature approved the commissioning of a new statue to honor women who had served in the military.

Once again, Mullins got the job of creating it. However, when he revealed the design in 2003, some people objected. They thought it was too muscular and not feminine enough. They suggested putting the woman in a skirt. Some wanted her to be recast to look like Private First Class Jessica Lynch, a Wirt County woman who had received national attention after having been held as a prisoner of war in Iraq. But Mullins said it was too late for that. His challenge had been to create one statue that would represent women who had served in all branches of the service during all wars. He said putting her in a skirt or a battle dress uniform or even fatigues could exclude some female veterans. To avoid that problem, he put her in combat boots, fatigue pants, an equipment belt with pouches, a T-shirt and a field cap over hair pulled into a bun. Putting even a blouse on her, he said, would have required identifying her branch or job title. Female veterans were divided on the issue.

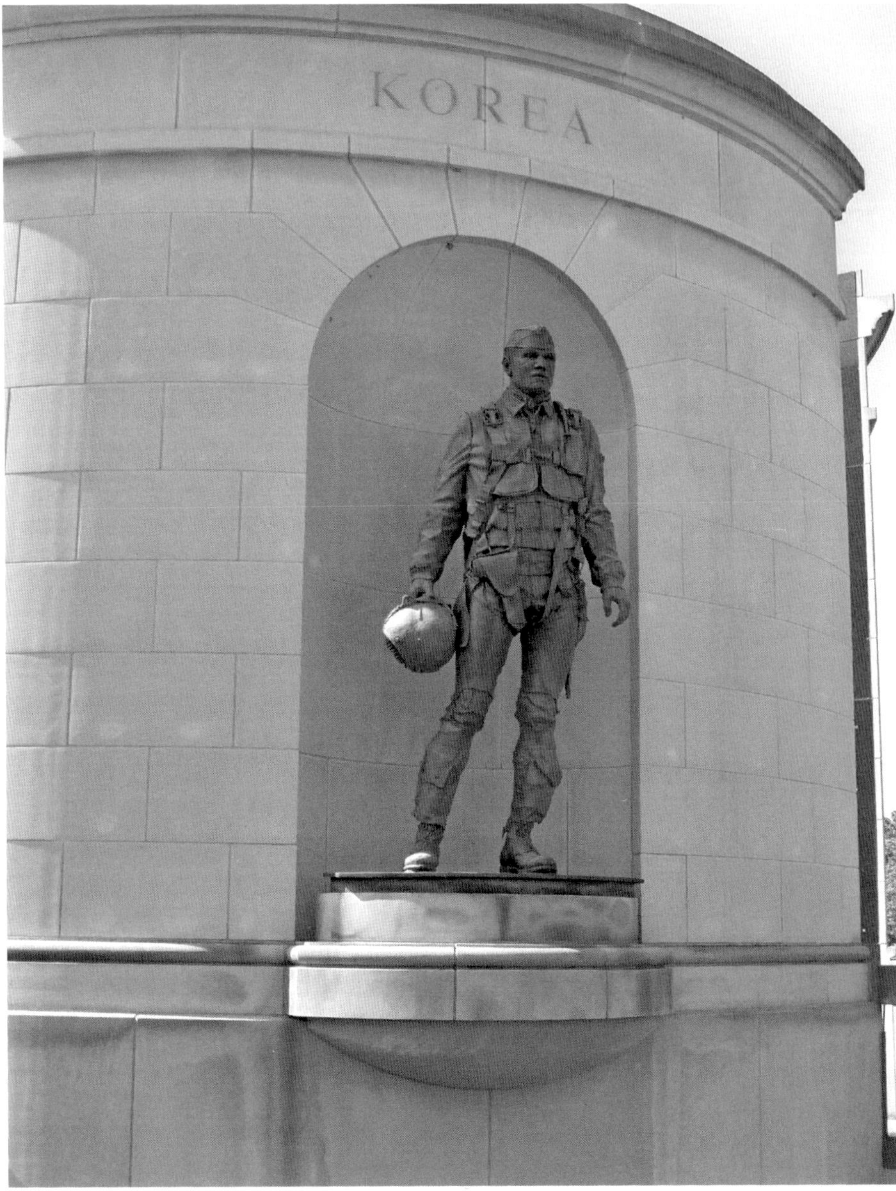

A Korean War airman statue represents U.S. Air Force veterans. *Photo by Jim Wallace.*

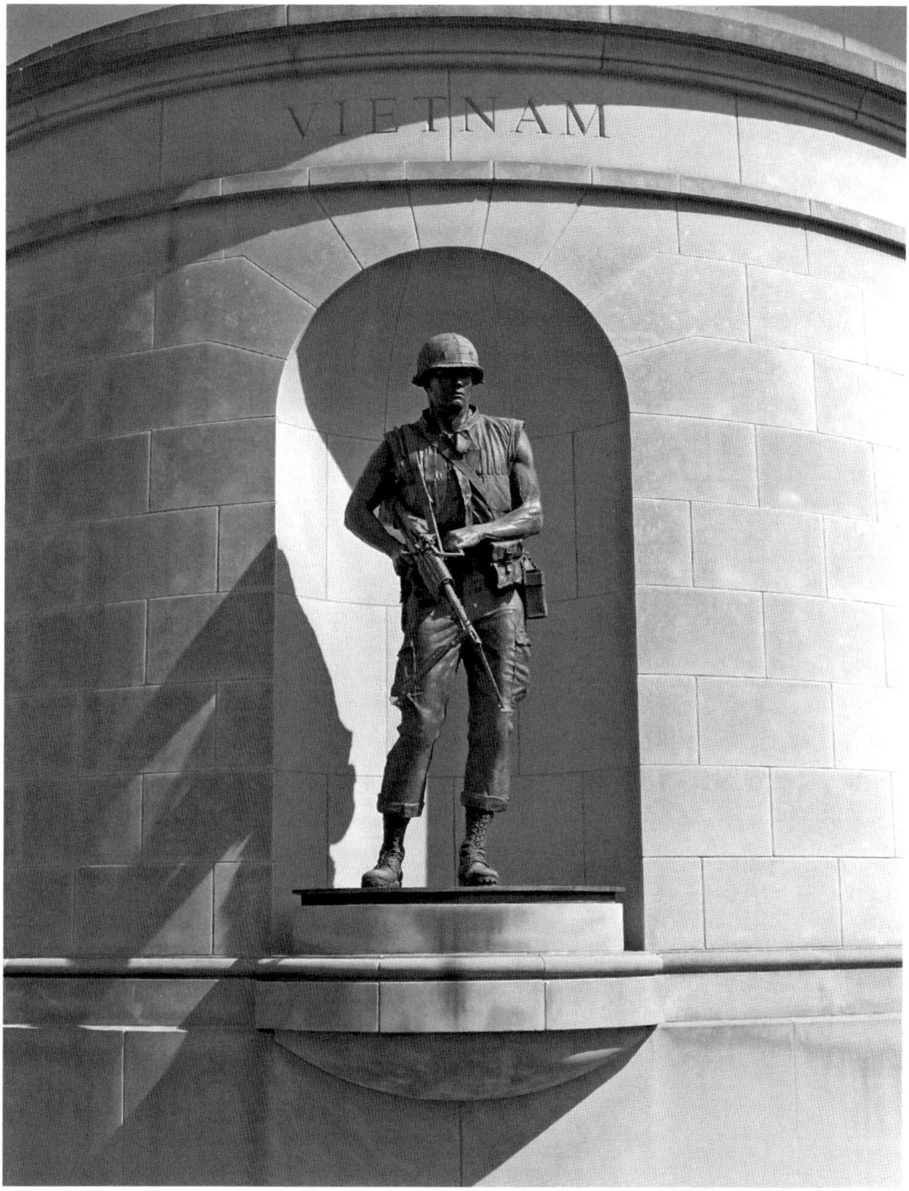

A Vietnam War marine statue represents U.S. Marine Corps veterans. *Photo by Jim Wallace.*

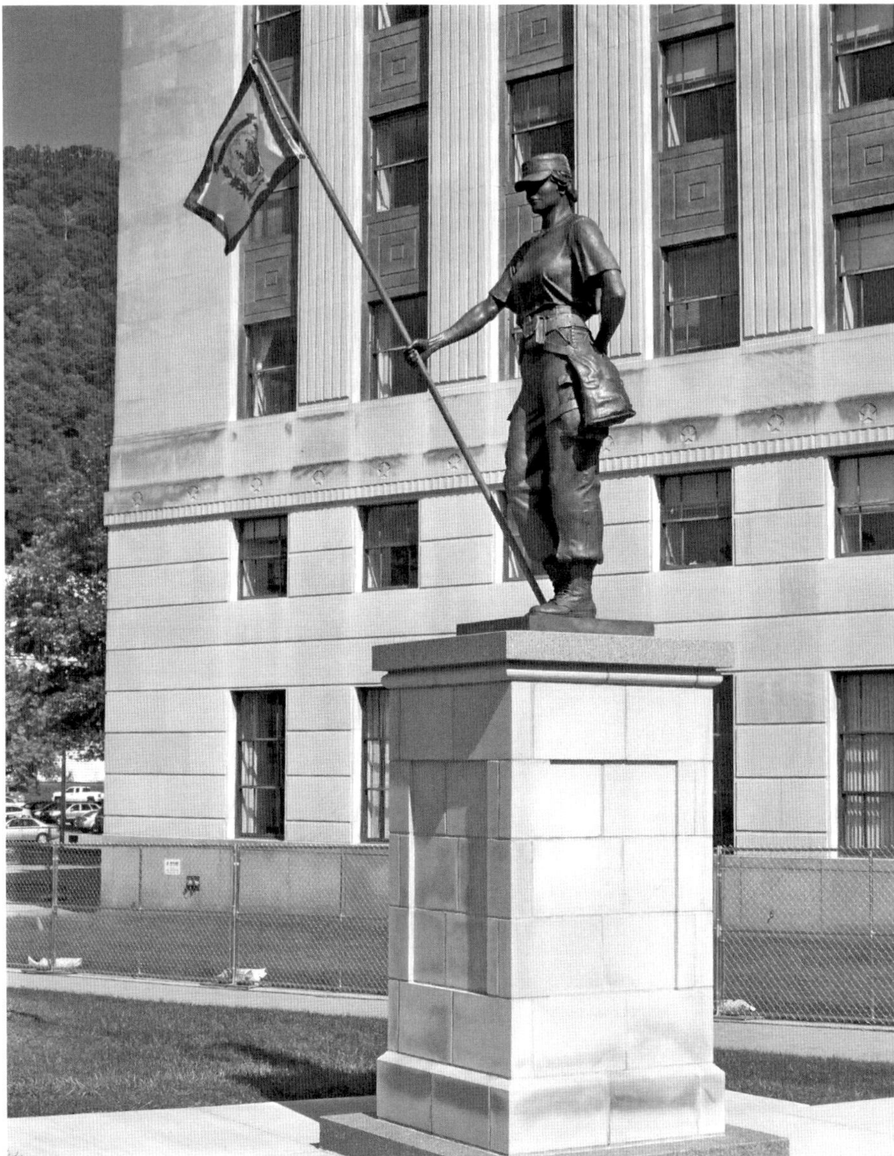

West Virginia's Female Veteran statue honors women from the state who have served in the military. *Photo by Jim Wallace.*

The controversy simmered for years. In 2005, a review committee set up by the Division of Veteran Affairs decided to abandon the design after a poll of female veterans found most of them opposed it. In 2006, a plan arose to place the statue at the state veterans' nursing home in Clarksburg instead of at the Capitol Complex. Mullins objected. The battle started going his way in 2008, when a new panel of female veterans approved the statue, but just barely. The vote was five to four. In 2009, the Capitol Building Commission gave its approval.

That autumn, the bronze statue, which stands seven feet and six inches tall and weighs about 750 pounds, was placed on a nine-foot-tall concrete base about fifty feet from the Veterans Memorial, midway between the memorial and Building 3, shortly before Veterans Day. It faces toward the memorial. But it took another two years before decorative plaques on the base were finished. The total cost was about $200,000. State officials dedicated it on Veterans Day 2011. In almost thirteen years since the legislature called for the statue to be commissioned, thousands of West Virginia women had become veterans of the wars in Afghanistan and Iraq.

OTHER PUBLIC SERVANTS

Two other statues stand on the balcony terrace on the northern side of the Culture Center.

One is *Fallen Partner*, a memorial to West Virginia law enforcement officers killed in the line of duty. It is a seven-foot statue on a four-foot-tall pedestal. The state lodge of the Fraternal Order of Police came up with the idea for it in 1986 and spent $70,000 to have sculptor Bill Hopen of Sutton create it. The officer portrayed in the statue wears a uniform meant to be a composite of all police forces in the state. His left hand holds a shield that says "PAX," which is Latin for "peace," as well as a scroll that is a symbol of law enforcement. He looks sadly down at his right hand, which carries a partner's gun belt and badge. When it was dedicated on May 19, 1990, the plaque on the pedestal contained the names of 107 officers who died on the job. Other names have been added since then.

The Fallen Partner statue received a companion a few years later, when the Fallen Firefighter Memorial joined it. The West Virginia Firefighters Association paid about $70,000 to have sculptor James Lykins of Elkview create the statue of a six-and-a-half-foot firefighter wearing a mask and

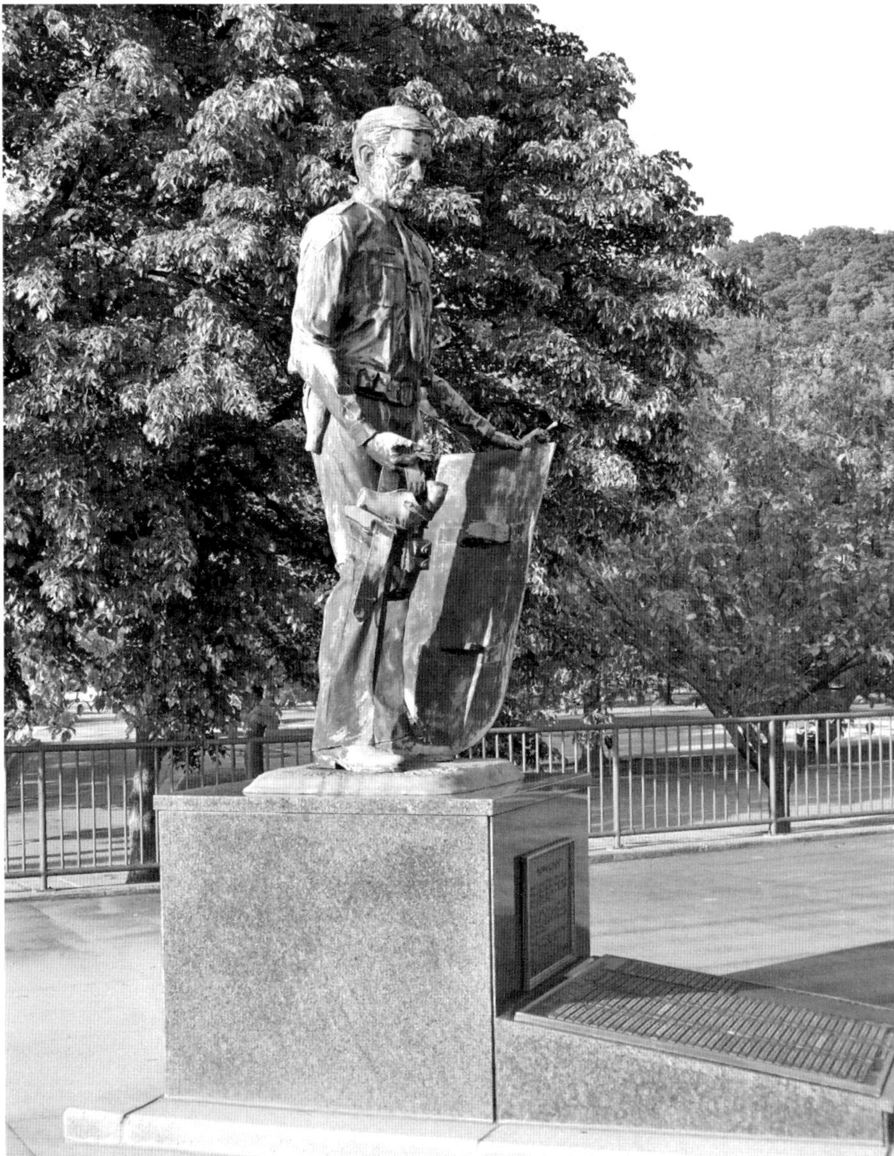

The *Fallen Partner* statue honors law enforcement officers killed in the line of duty. *Photo by Jim Wallace.*

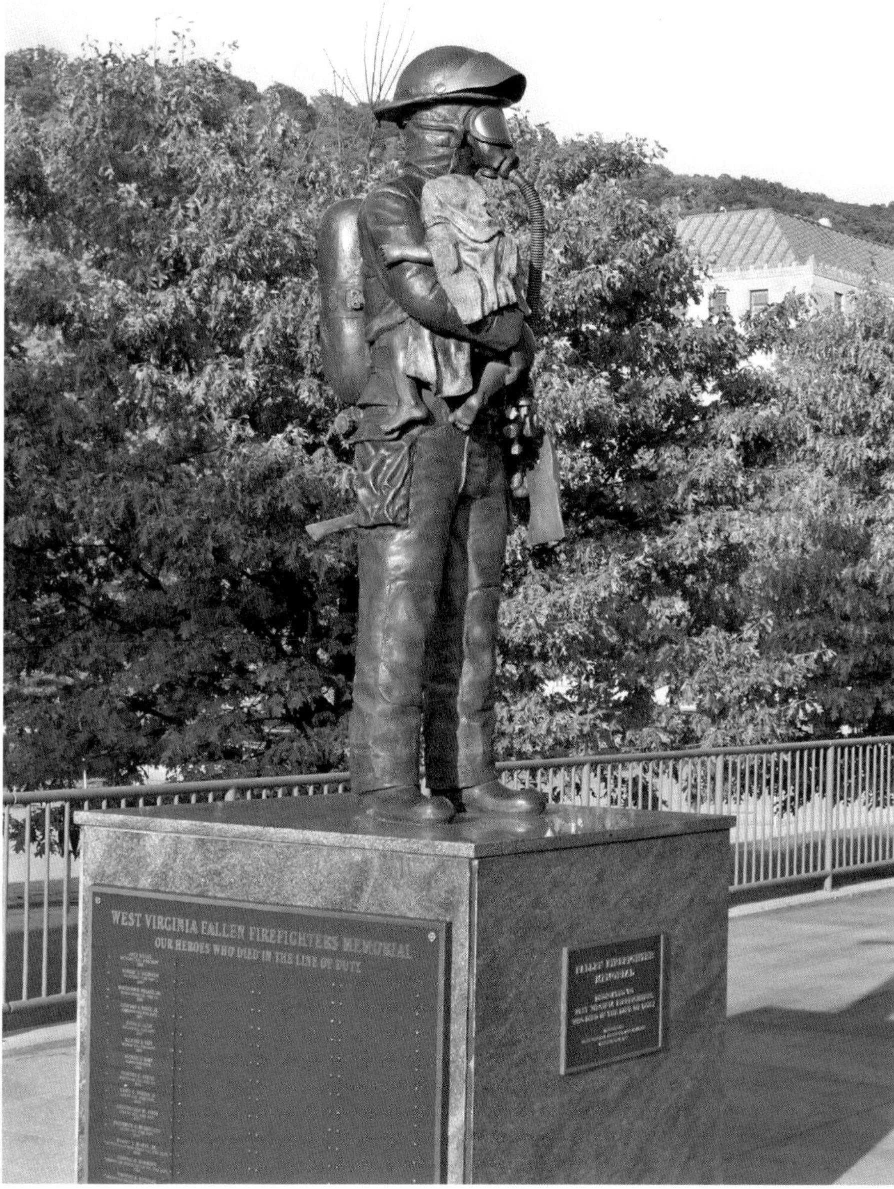

The *Fallen Firefighter Memorial* honors West Virginia firefighters who have died in the line of duty. *Photo by Jim Wallace.*

carrying a small child wrapped in a blanket in one hand and an ax in the other. It was dedicated on September 9, 1994, to honor West Virginia firefighters who died in the line of duty. Later, a plaque was added that listed all the firefighters who had died while on duty since 1900.

COAL'S ROLE

Across from the Culture Center and near the west wing of the Capitol is the *West Virginia Coal Miner* statue that pays tribute to the state's coal-mining heritage. It is a bronze statue created by Burl Jones of Kanawha County. The miner is seven feet and six inches tall. Jones said he used his father-in-law, Russell Holmes, who owned a mining business, as inspiration for the statue. The miner wears a hard hat and overalls. He has a lantern, an electric light, a battery pack and a survival kit.

The statue stands on a six-sided black marble pedestal that is five feet high. It bears the title on the front, credits on the back and bas-relief plaques on the other sides. Those plaques depict different periods of mining and the technologies used to extract coal, ranging from picks and axes to modern machines for continuous mining, long-wall mining and surface mining. Jones suggested adding the plaques to resolve a dispute over whether the statue should depict a modern miner, as it does, or one from the early days of mining. But another controversy arose when environmental advocates objected to the panel depicting surface mining, or what they called mountaintop removal mining. They said that and a reference to coal as a cheap source of energy were propaganda for the coal industry, but they were unsuccessful in getting it changed.

The legislature authorized the statue in 1999. The Capitol Building Commission approved the design based on a scale model Jones presented in 2001. The $150,000 for the statue came mostly from private donors, including the coal industry and the United Mine Workers.

Governor Bob Wise led the dedication ceremony for the statue on March 6, 2003. The crowd included several hundred miners, coal truckers and others who supported the coal industry.

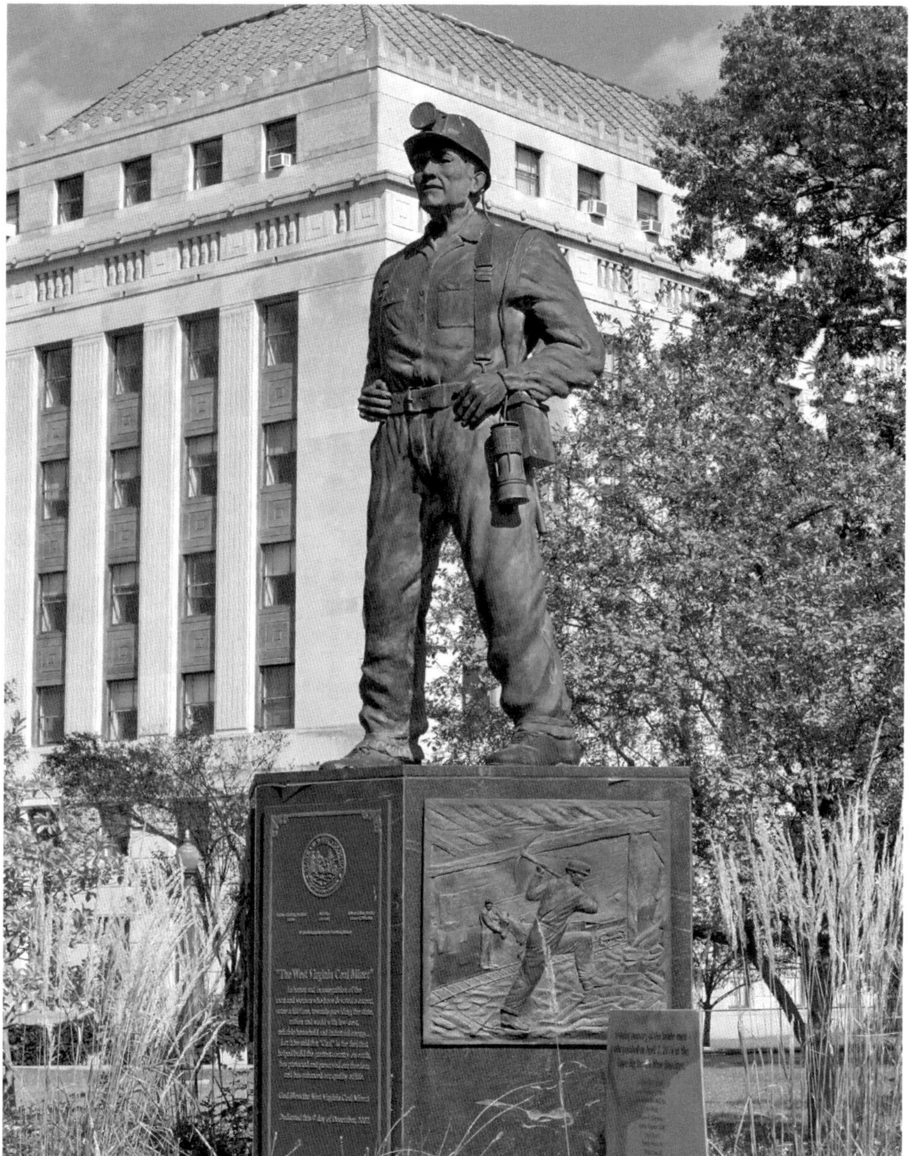

The *West Virginia Coal Miner* statue honors people who have served in one of the state's most important industries. *Photo by Jim Wallace.*

BELL AND TREES

The Liberty Bell stands north of the Capitol Circle in the courtyard between the east and west wings of the Capitol. It is one of fifty-three bells cast in France and given to the U.S. government. The bell is identical to the original Liberty Bell in Philadelphia. West Virginia received it in 1950 as part of a commemoration of a drive for U.S. Savings Bonds.

The grounds of the Capitol Complex include, by one count, more than five hundred trees—many of them large and old—including such species as elm, holly, cedar, crab apple, oak, pine and sugar maple, which is the official state tree. But two younger trees get special attention. One is an American elm planted as a five-foot-tall sapling in 2008 along the walk outside the west side entrance to the Capitol. The sapling came from the so-called Survivor Tree that was damaged but not destroyed by the April 19, 1995 bombing of the Alfred P. Murrah Federal Building in Oklahoma City. It was five feet tall when Kim Henry, Oklahoma's first lady, presented it to Gayle Manchin, who then was West Virginia's first lady. It is expected to grow to be about eighty feet tall.

The other is a chestnut tree along the walkway that leads from Greenbrier Street to the west side of the Capitol. The tree is near the guardhouse that vehicles must pass to get into the parking lot near the Governor's Mansion. The plaque in the ground next to the tree calls it "The Restoration Chestnut" and says it was planted in memory of the Upper Big Branch miners who perished on April 5, 2010. That is a reference to the twenty-nine miners who died from an explosion at that mine, which was owned by Massey Coal, near Montcoal in Raleigh County. It was the worst coal-mining disaster in the country in almost forty years. The West Virginia Chapter of the American Chestnut Foundation presented the tree to the state. The foundation is trying to restore the American chestnut in several states by using a blight-resistant strain of the species. A fungal infection almost wiped out the species in the early twentieth century.

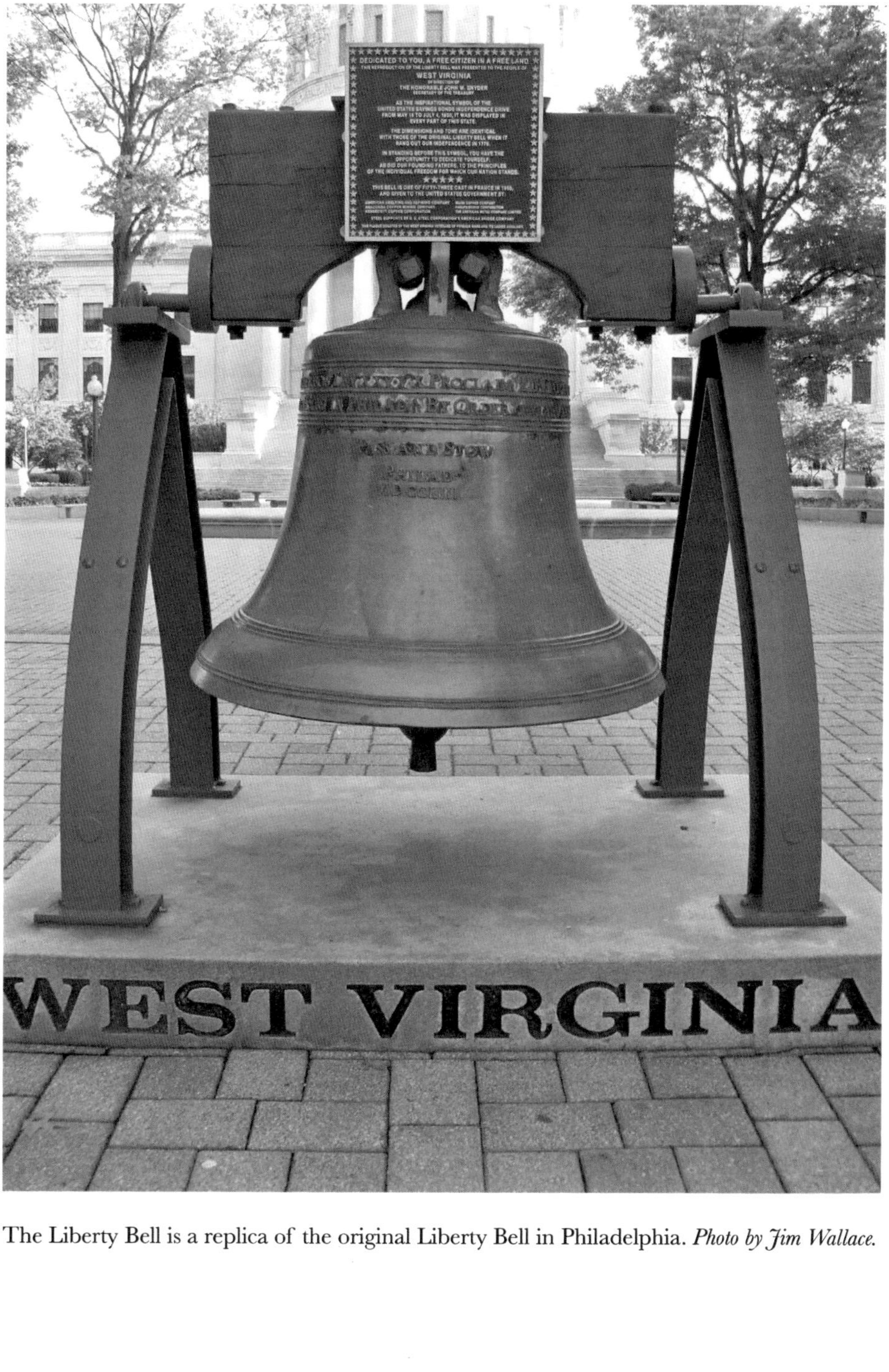

The Liberty Bell is a replica of the original Liberty Bell in Philadelphia. *Photo by Jim Wallace.*

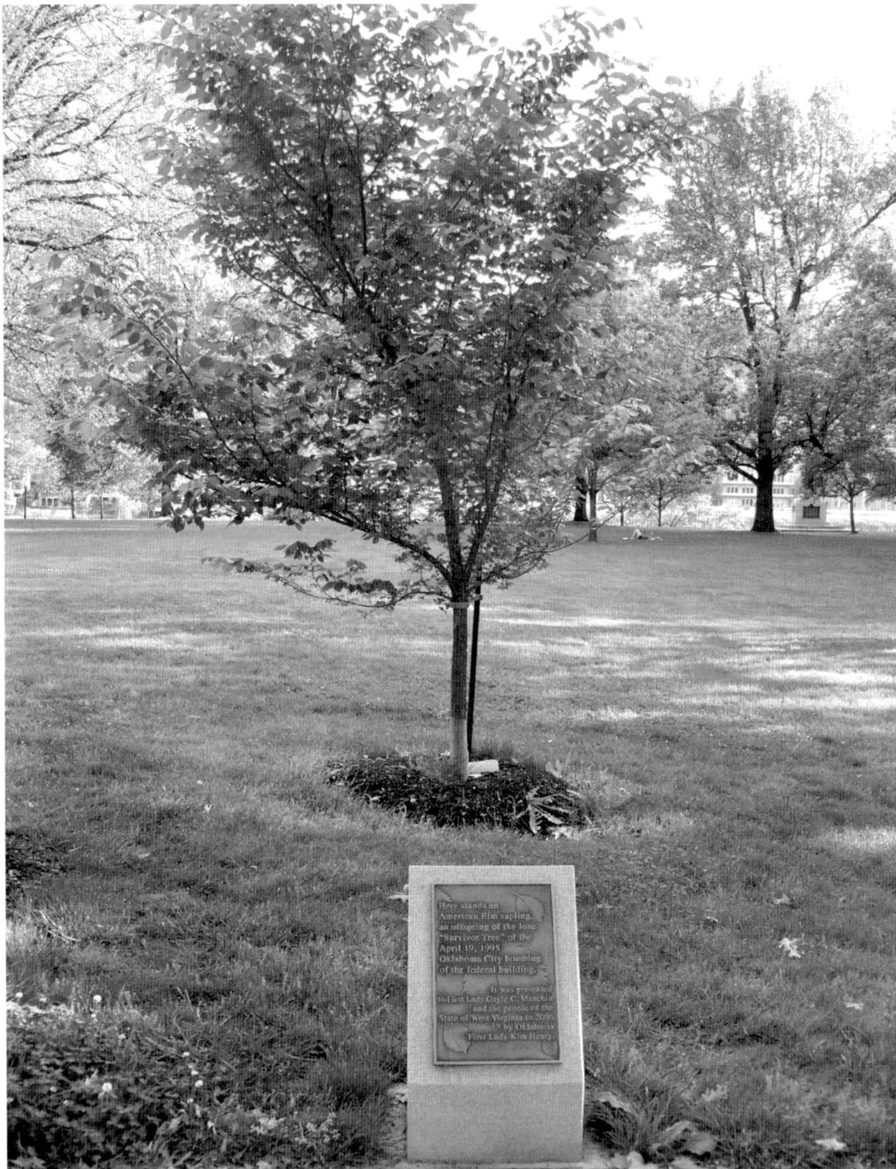

The Survivor Tree is a memorial to people who died in the 1995 bombing of the federal building in Oklahoma City. *Photo by Jim Wallace.*

BYRD'S PLACE

Most of the Capitol's statues have been placed on the grounds outside of the building, even though Cass Gilbert incorporated into his design several places for statues inside the building. Those places include alcoves on the second floor around the main rotunda, as well as alcoves in the smaller rotundas on the western and eastern sides of the first floor of the Capitol's main unit. However, so far, only one statue has been placed in one of those alcoves.

A ten-foot-tall bronze statue of Senator Robert Byrd, weighing 1,500 pounds, stands in the northwestern alcove on the second floor of the rotunda. It depicts Byrd holding in his left hand a section of the U.S. Constitution that gives Congress the authority to appropriate taxpayers' money, because Byrd had used his positions in the Senate, particularly as chairman of the Appropriations Committee, to bring West Virginia more than $1.5 billion in federal funding for projects from new roads to office buildings. His right hand is extended downward with its index finger pointing, as Byrd might have done during one of his many speeches over his long career.

Planning for the statue began in 1994. Byrd was present for its unveiling on January 11, 1997, in a ceremony led by Governor Gaston Caperton, who was completing his second term. Byrd's colleague Senator Jay Rockefeller was also among the many dignitaries present for the ceremony. Byrd said he hoped the statue would "serve as a beacon for anyone who may aspire to achievement." By the time the statue was dedicated, Byrd had served more than fifty years in public office, beginning in the West Virginia Legislature and moving on to the U.S. House of Representatives and then the U.S. Senate. In 2006, he became the longest-serving member of the Senate, and in 2009, he became the longest-serving member of Congress. Byrd served in the Senate up until his death at age ninety-two in 2010. A plaque at the base of the statue calls Byrd the "West Virginian of the twentieth century," a title conferred on him by the state legislature. Bill Hopen of Sutton created the statue. About $100,000 in donations paid for it.

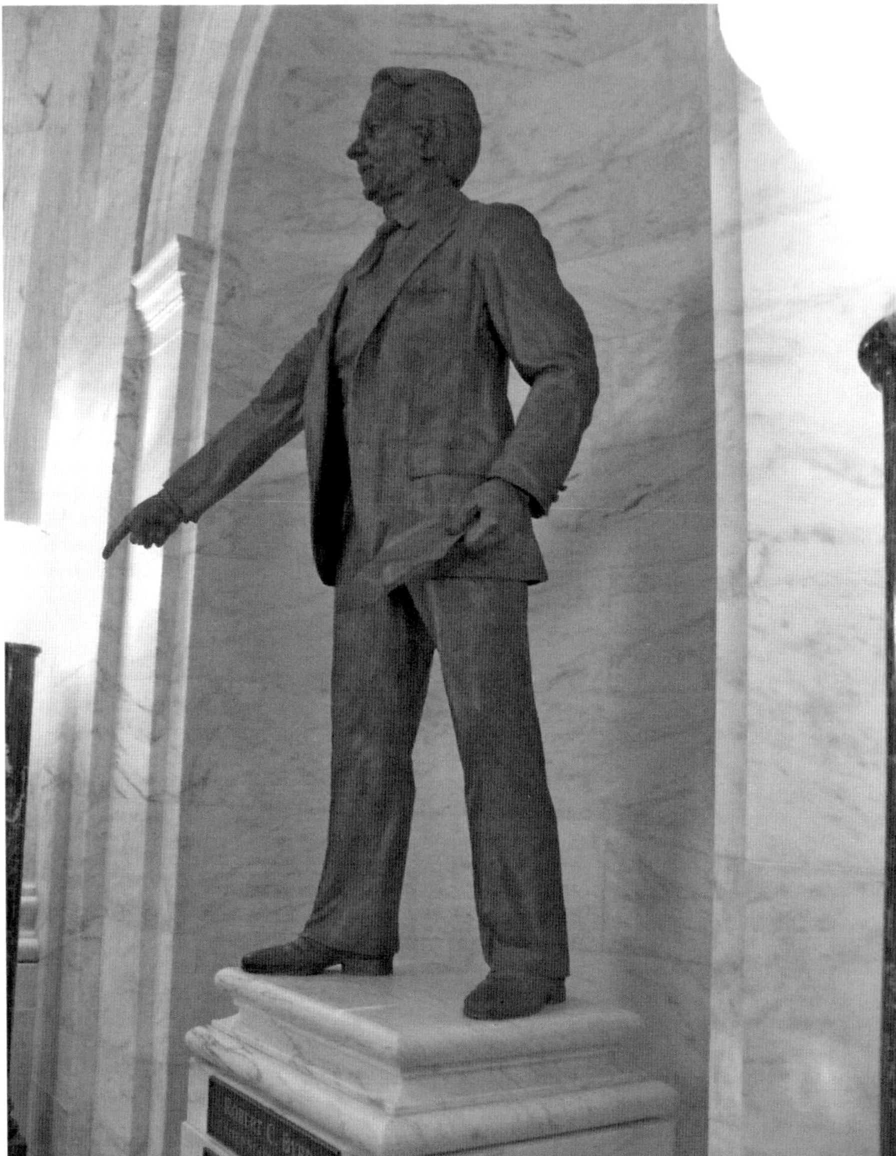

The statue of Senator Robert Byrd was the first statue to be placed in the Capitol's rotunda, although Cass Gilbert had made room for many more inside the building. *Photo by Jim Wallace.*

BUSTS

The busts of three notable West Virginians sit on pedestals on the ground floor of the rotunda. Two of them are near the marble stairways that lead to the second floor.

Apparently, a statue on the Capitol lawn was not enough for the United Daughters of the Confederacy to demonstrate their admiration for Stonewall Jackson, because the bust near the eastern stairway is also of him. The West Virginia division of the organization presented it to the state in 1959. The pedestal describes Jackson as a "military genius," a "brave soldier" and a "noble Christian."

Near the western stairway is a bronze bust of Cleve Bailey, who lived from 1886 to 1965 and served eight terms in the U.S. House of Representatives from what then was the third congressional district, which at the time included central West Virginia counties from Harrison to Fayette. He served from 1945 to 1947 and then from 1949 to 1963. Bailey worked to protect the jobs of West Virginia workers from foreign competition. The pedestal of the bust states that members of organized labor presented it to the state "for his devotion to the cause of education and labor during sixteen years of distinguished and dedicated service in the Congress of the United States."

On the opposite side of the lower rotunda is a bust of Anna Jarvis, the Taylor County woman who was the founder of Mother's Day and a keynote speaker during the Capitol's dedication ceremony in 1932. Lorna Vincent-Venter of Grafton sculpted the bust of bonded bronze. The Thunder on the Tygart Foundation, a nonprofit organization dedicated to historic preservation, commissioned the bust. The foundation, based in Grafton, also restored the Anna Jarvis Birthplace Museum in Webster. A ceremony to dedicate the bust was held at the Capitol on November 9, 2001. Jarvis became the first woman to be so honored at the Capitol. The only other monument representing a woman on the Capitol grounds is the *Female Veteran* statue, which depicts a generic woman rather than a specific woman.

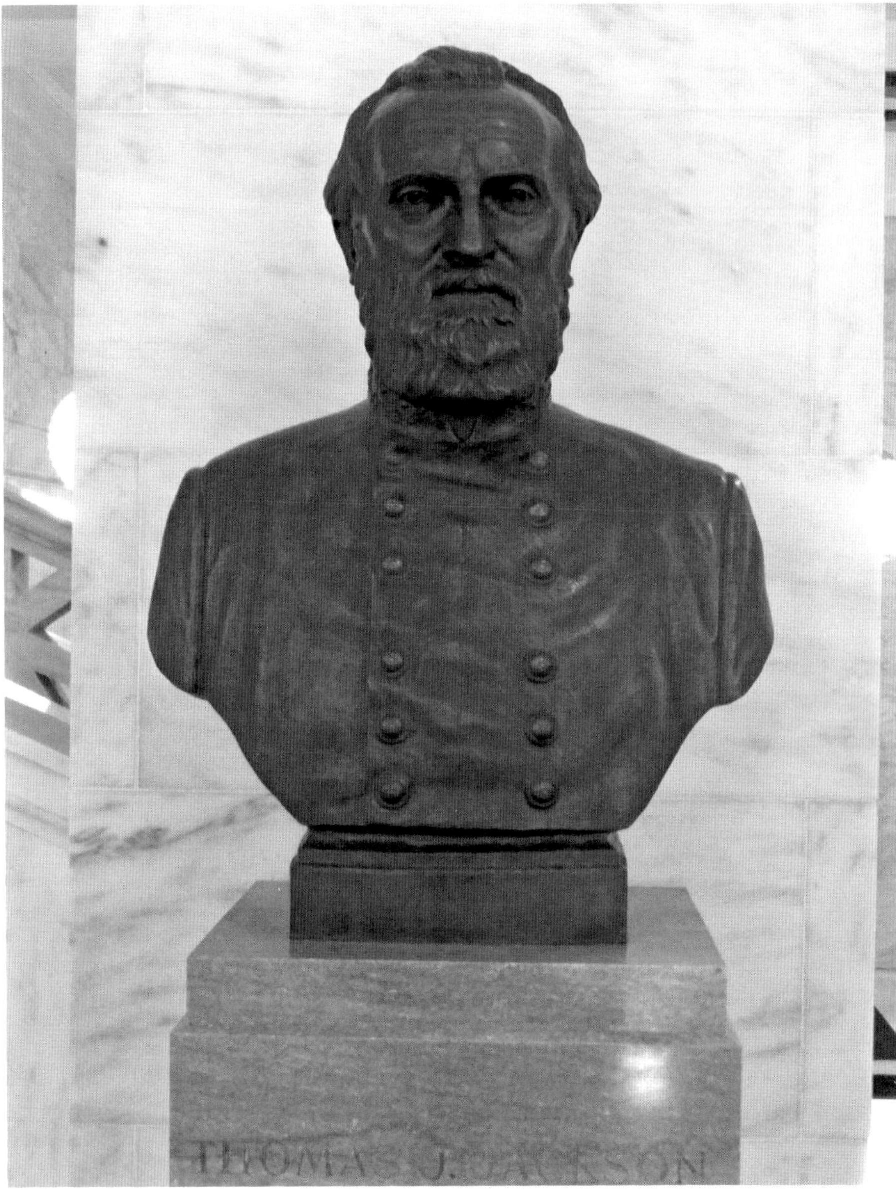

Stonewall Jackson is the only person to be represented not only by a statue outside the Capitol but also by a bust inside. *Photo by Jim Wallace.*

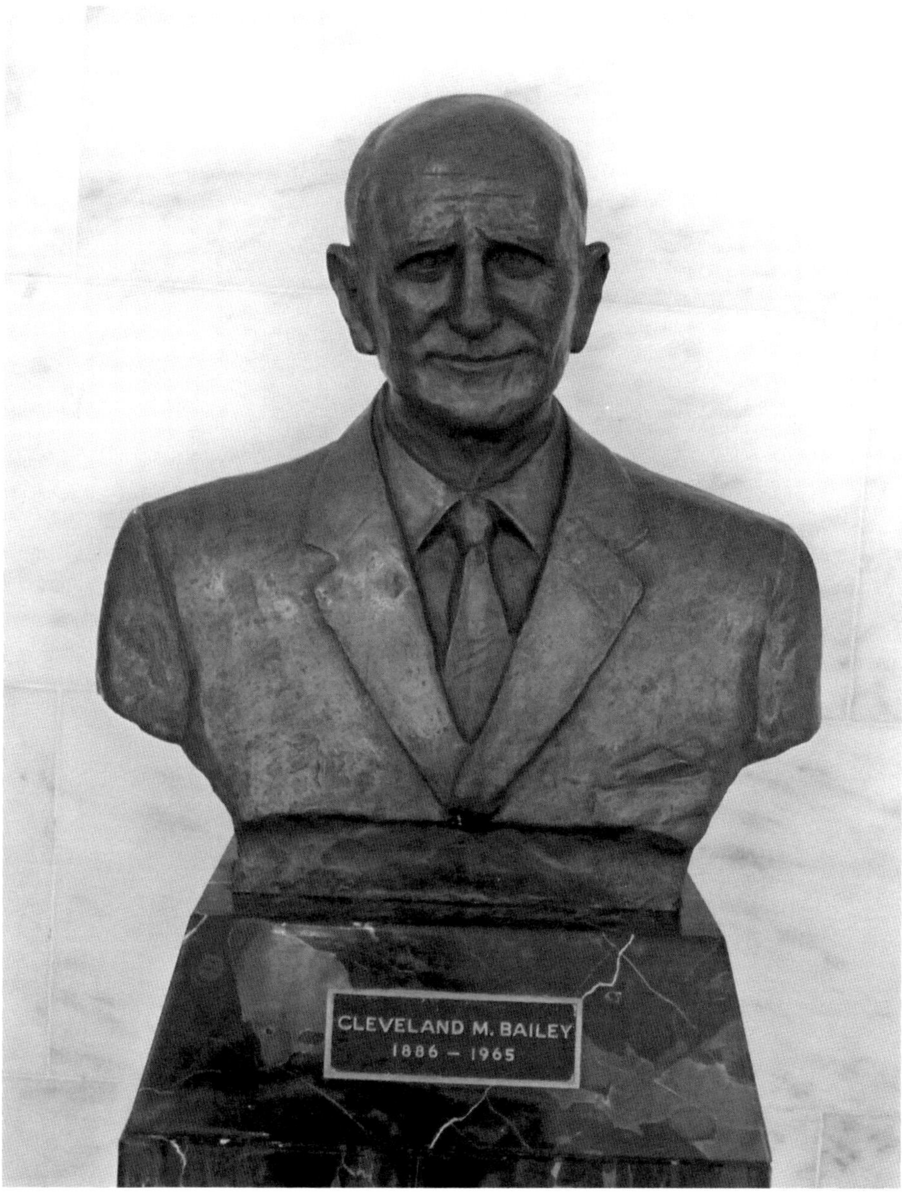

Cleve Bailey, a congressman beloved by the labor movement, is represented by a bust on the ground floor of the Capitol. *Photo by Jim Wallace.*

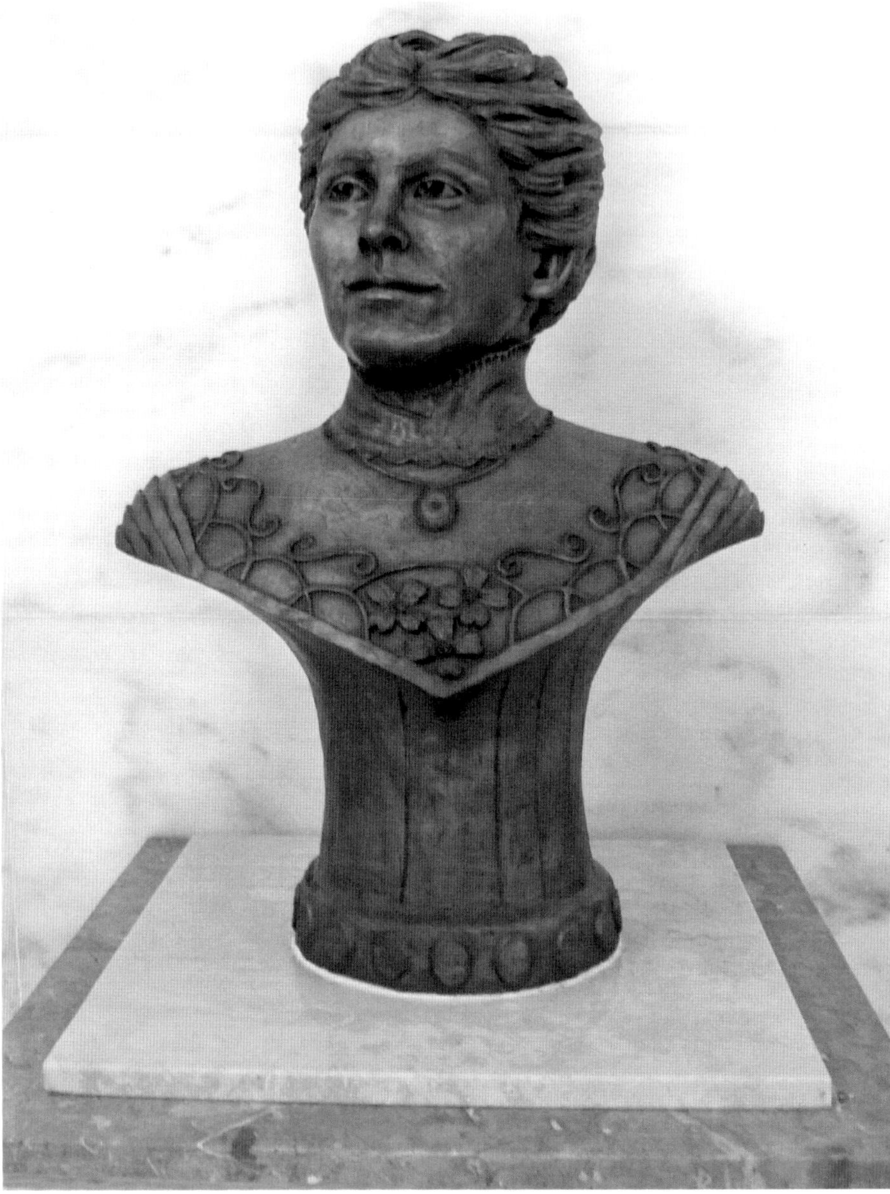

The bust of Anna Jarvis honors the founder of Mother's Day. *Photo by Jim Wallace.*

GOVERNORS IN THE HALLS

Anyone who wants a quick review of the governors of West Virginia need only walk through the ground floor of the Capitol, where each one is represented by a framed portrait. The portrait of the first governor, Arthur Boreman, hangs in the hallway not far from the western entrance to the Capitol, between the offices for the governor and the secretary of state. The portraits of subsequent governors follow in order down the hallway to the eastern end and then back. The only two portraits not in the hallway are those of the two most recent former governors, which hang in the governor's reception room. The most recent former governor's portrait hangs nearest to the governor's inner office. That has resulted in situations in which the portrait of a governor defeated for reelection hangs over events presided over by the governor who defeated him. For example, Arch Moore's portrait hung in the reception room throughout the administration of Gaston Caperton, and Cecil Underwood's portrait hung there during the administration of Bob Wise.

Underwood is the only person to have two portraits, one depicting him as West Virginia's youngest governor from 1957 to 1961 and one as the oldest governor from 1997 to 2001. He was thirty-four at his first inauguration, seventy-four at his second and seventy-eight when he left office. Moore, the other governor who served nonconsecutive terms, decided not to have a new portrait painted after his third term ended. He served two terms from 1969 to 1977 and one more term from 1985 to 1989.

Sometimes, governors arrange to have their portraits painted before they leave office. That is true for governors such as Rockefeller and Caperton, who served two consecutive terms and knew because of term limits when they would leave office, and Wise, who decided not to seek a second term. When a governor who hopes to serve another term is defeated for reelection, there can be a delay in getting the portrait done. For example, Underwood's second portrait was unveiled in September 2001, eight months after he left office. A longer delay developed after Joe Manchin won a special election in 2010 to assume the late Robert Byrd's U.S. Senate seat with more than two years left in his second term. At the time this book was written in mid-2012, Manchin still did not have his portrait hanging in the Capitol.

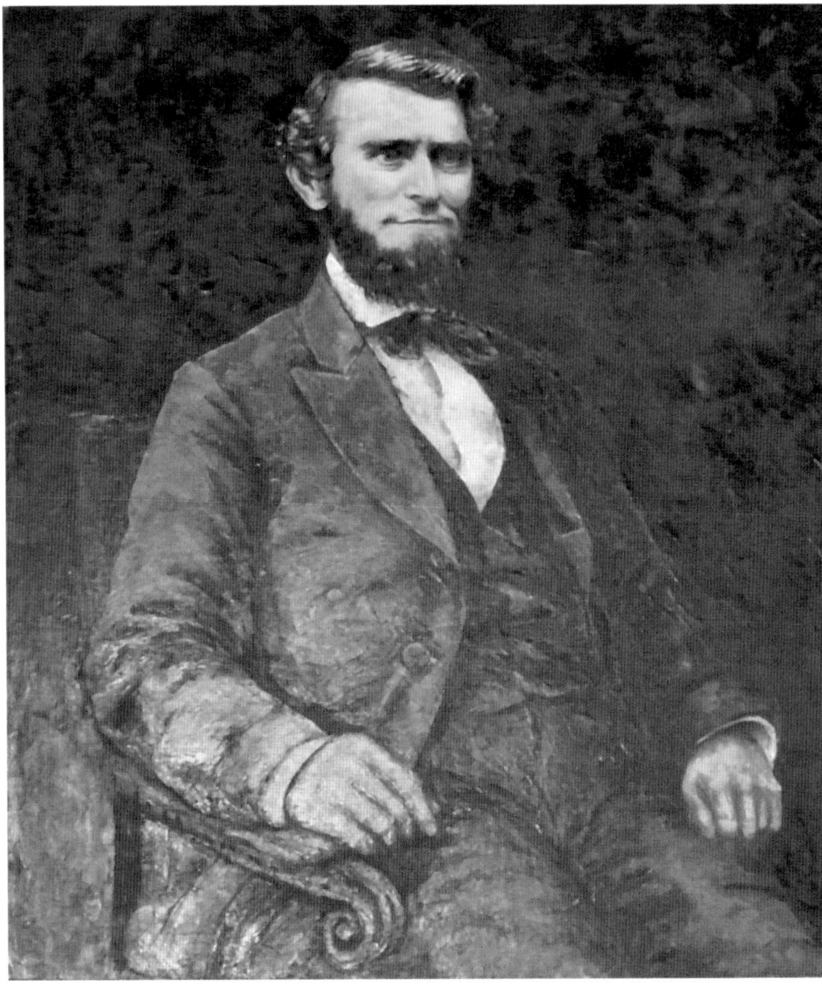

Arthur Boreman, West Virginia's first governor, is also the first of the state's many governors whose portraits are displayed consecutively in the hallway on the ground floor of the Capitol. *Photo by Jim Wallace.*

CAPITOLS THROUGH THE YEARS

Although most of the alcoves in the Capitol have not been filled with statues, as Cass Gilbert had wanted, those in the small rotundas on the western end near the governor's office and on the eastern end near the attorney general's office have been used in recent years for historical displays of photos of all

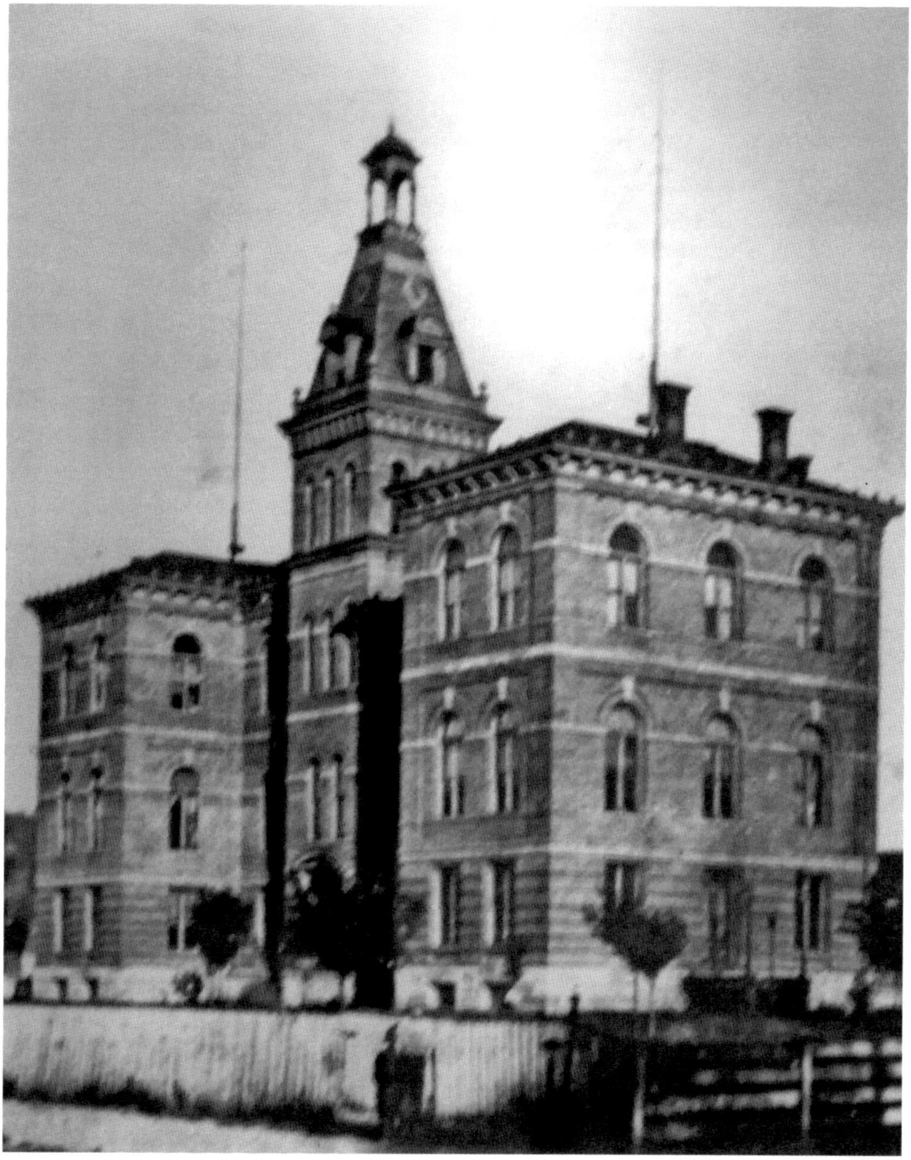

This is a copy of the only known photograph of the first Capitol built in Charleston. It is among several photos displayed in the small rotundas on the western and eastern ends of the ground floor of the current Capitol. *Photo by Jim Wallace.*

of West Virginia's Capitols. One of the four alcoves on the west side displays the only known photo of the first Capitol built in Charleston. In the other three alcoves are photos of West Virginia Independence Hall (seat of the so-called Restored Government of Virginia), the Linsly Institute building used as the first Capitol in Wheeling and the second Capitol that was built in Wheeling. In the alcoves on the east side are photos of the second Capitol built in Charleston, the "Pasteboard" Capitol that was used after the second Charleston Capitol burned, the Capitol Annex that once housed some government agencies in downtown Charleston and the current Capitol.

BEARS

Another display on the first floor of the Capitol, near that small rotunda on the east side, does not commemorate a building or a person but another type of West Virginian: the black bear. It has been recognized as the state animal since a poll conducted in 1954–55 in which West Virginians—including many students, teachers and outdoor enthusiasts—chose the black bear by a wide margin over other candidates for that honor. In 1973, the legislature passed a resolution to make it official. But it took more than a decade after that decision before a stuffed bear went on display in the Capitol.

Ken Hechler, a Democrat who had served in President Harry Truman's White House and later represented a West Virginia district in the U.S. House of Representatives for eighteen years, acquired the first bear after he became secretary of state in 1985. He already had decorated his Capitol office with paintings of state symbols, including the state bird (cardinal), tree (sugar maple), fish (brook trout), flower (rhododendron) and animal (black bear), as well as the state seal, but he wanted more. So on January 14, 1986, Hechler had four men deliver to his office a five-foot-tall stuffed black bear.

The Department of Natural Resources had killed the bear in 1984 in Clay County near the border with Nicholas County. Hechler told the *Charleston Daily Mail* that the department decided the bear, which was five years old and weighed about three hundred pounds, had to be killed because he was scaring residents in that area. "He was getting into a lot of people's beehives and fooling around in landfills and dumps and trying to pick up extra food where people were," Hechler said. He arranged to buy it through a state surplus property auction. The bear became especially popular with children who visited the Capitol. Hechler encouraged them to pet it.

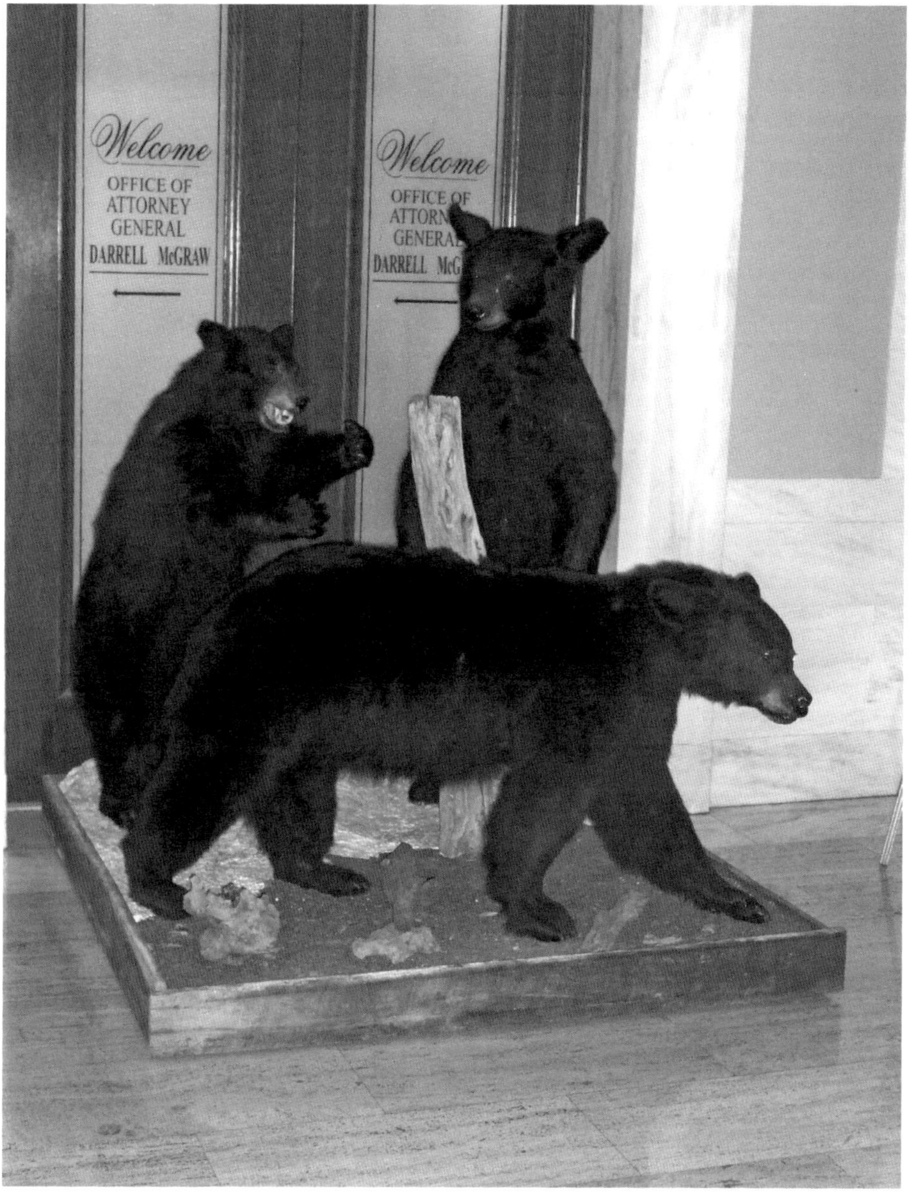

The black bear, West Virginia's state animal, has been represented in the Capitol since 1986, first by one bear at the secretary of state's office and now by three in front of the attorney general's office. *Photo by Jim Wallace.*

But all that handling was rough on the bear. By the early 1990s, it had lost much of its hair. Hechler planned to replace it with a second bear, but the taxidermist was able to restore the first bear while also stuffing the second one. The first bear was posed rearing up on his hind legs, so the taxidermist posed the second bear standing on all four legs. Hechler told the *Daily Mail* in 1994 that he did not learn about the background of the second bear. He said he paid $600 to $800 of his own money to buy each bear hide at state surplus property auctions and about $300 to have each one stuffed.

In a poke of fun at gun rights activists, Hechler put up a sign around one bear's neck with a twist on the Constitution's Second Amendment right to bear arms. It stated: "We support the right to arm bears."

Although he once said he would donate the bears to his successor, Hechler changed his mind in 2000, as he entered the final months of his last term as secretary of state. Joe Manchin, who was the leading candidate to succeed Hechler and later the winner of that November's election, had announced that he would sell the bears and use the proceeds for voters' registration efforts. The Division of Culture and History rejected Hechler's offer to donate them to the agency, but he entertained more than thirty offers from people who wanted him to donate the bears or sell them. That October, he accepted an offer from Attorney General Darrell McGraw, a fellow Democrat who was unopposed for reelection. McGraw agreed to display the bears just outside of his office on the east side of the Capitol. Just before Hechler left office in January 2001, the bears were wheeled down the hallway to McGraw's office. They have remained there since then and even acquired a third companion, which, like the first one, is posed standing on its hind legs.

Chapter 9

Preserving the Heritage

Cass Gilbert long has been revered in West Virginia for the masterpiece of a Capitol he designed. Over the decades, his name has often been invoked when there are issues over how to maintain the Capitol or augment it. Essentially, people's concerns have been some form of the question: What would Gilbert have wanted?

Well, one thing that he wanted was for the state to take good care of the Capitol. In his 1932 letter to *Charleston Daily Mail* editor Walter Clark, Gilbert called maintenance and upkeep "really an important matter." He recommended that the Capitol should be placed under a permanent, nonpolitical body to oversee its upkeep and predicted some of the problems that would later develop when his advice was not followed:

> *Every building, like a ship, needs some upkeep. Heat and frost cause expansion and contraction, joints of masonry open and shut, roofing likewise, and woodwork shrinks and swells and needs occasional attention. Even the best of locks and fixtures occasionally get out of order, drain outlets become stopped up by careless usage, accumulations of inflammable rubbish are placed in basements or attics, grounds are defaced by improper planting and by the location of monuments or statues at unsuitable points; even cast iron vases and cast iron deer and dogs have been placed in geranium beds, and the active but untutored fancy of a garden employee has sometimes defaced the best of landscape plans. These and many other*

> *things too numerous to cite, and almost too remote to imagine, have occurred to public buildings and grounds, all of which, under proper direction, would have been avoided.*

Even though many state officials have expressed interest in preserving Gilbert's vision, the Capitol has not always been maintained as well as it should have. At times, conditions have become so bad that chunks of stone or ceiling have fallen or were in danger of falling, which could have been lethal to anyone unlucky enough to be directly underneath at the wrong time. Even worse, there have been times when maintenance had been put off for so long that it was feared that a strong wind could have blown the dome off of the building or that the central section of the building could have collapsed. Imagine how that could have damaged West Virginia's reputation. Fortunately, years of neglect have been followed by years of repairs, renovations and renewal of Gilbert's vision, sometimes seemingly just in time.

THE GOLDEN ISSUE

The Capitol's most prominent feature, the dome, has also been the subject of some of the most prominent battles over the decades: to gild or not to gild. That has been the question—many times.

As the architect, Gilbert had to fight the first battle. When critics contended that gilding was an unnecessary extravagance, Gilbert had to convince the Capitol Building Commission that it not only would be better aesthetically but also cheaper in the long run, because it would require less maintenance than paint.

But both alternatives had problems. In 1931, the same year the gold leaf was first applied, Bonner Hill, the commission's secretary, noticed spots on the surface of the dome, as well as dirt against its ornaments. Gilbert inspected the problems himself during several trips to Charleston. After one of those trips, Hill wrote to him, "I trust you saw the spots on the ribs of the Capitol dome where, if there was ever any gold leaf, the scaffold destroyed it." Gilbert maintained confidence in Mack, Jenny and Tyler, the company with the contract for the gilding. But he responded to Hill, "If it is found that the areas have not been covered with gold leaf, the contractor should be required to do the work without expense to the state, including the cost of the scaffold." Although Gilbert expected the gold to last twenty years, it was in bad shape within six years.

By then, the gilding became the concern of Cass Gilbert Jr., who took over after his father died in 1934. A chemical analysis he commissioned in 1937 led to the conclusion that air and water, which had gotten between the lead of the dome and the gold leaf, were to blame for the problems, and they were perhaps exacerbated by sulfuric acid put into the Kanawha Valley's air by local chemical plants and factories. But in a 1940 letter, an official from DuPont, which operated one of those nearby plants, wrote, "We have a great deal of lead equipment in our heavy chemicals plants which is continually exposed to weak sulphuric acid, and this lead equipment lasts for years." He suggested the problem might lie in the daytime expansion and nighttime contraction of the lead and advised Gilbert to consult with lead companies. In 1941, Gilbert received proposals to clean the dome and gild it again—including one from Mack, Jenny and Tyler—but nothing was done with the dome until after World War II.

In 1946, the state had the gold removed and the dome painted, but within five years, the paint began to fail. As the state's centennial approached in 1963, officials decided to put a gold-and-blue enamel finish on the dome in time for the celebration.

By the mid-1970s, the dome needed more than just a new covering. Governor Arch Moore wanted to have it regilded, but before that could be done, the state had to spend about $100,000 on structural repairs to the dome. Although Moore's administration, in 1976, awarded a $472,000 contract to put gold leaf on the dome, it could not be done before Moore left office. The new governor, Jay Rockefeller, who came into office in 1977, cancelled the gilding, sold the gold and had the dome repainted gold and blue instead. Rockefeller figured he saved the state about $100,000. He put most of that money toward a new snowplow for Preston County.

Once again, the paint did not last. Within a few years, the blue began to peel, and the gold faded to yellow. By the mid-1980s, the metal of the dome was exposed to the elements, and there were fears that structural damage could result. The state called in Swanke Hayden Connell Architects, which had experience in projects around the world, including the restoration of the Statue of Liberty. That company determined that the problems with coating the dome with either gold leaf or paint came from trying to put it on the lead surface.

Again, the issue was whether to repaint or gild the dome. Moore—once again—was governor, and he still favored gilding, but he could not get it done without more controversy. When state officials opened bids for the job in December 1986, about two dozen protesters objected, saying the money should be used to help people who were unemployed, hungry or homeless. Despite that, the process moved forward. The lowest bid came in for $469,347. The company that made the bid said painting the dome would have cost just $42,000 less.

After seeing the first squares of gold applied to the dome in November 1988, a *Charleston Daily Mail* editorial writer proclaimed Rockefeller's 1977 decision not to gild the dome "simply the most foolish thing he did as governor." The writer further said, "Although he surely did not intend such a result, Rockefeller's decision to paint the dome made West Virginians look like hicks, unable to appreciate the beauty of Gilbert's masterpiece and incapable of taking care of it. That's a high price to pay for a snowplow for Preston County."

Yet again, Moore's term as governor—his third—ran out before he could see the dome fully covered with gold. Emmanuel Tsitsilianos, a Greek-born contractor in charge of the project, had decided that the job required not 23.0-carat gold but 23.5-carat gold because of environmental conditions. Later, that became 23.9-carat gold. That change delayed completion of the project, so when Moore left office in January 1989, the dome was only partially gilded. It did not fully gleam with gold until late in 1990, well into the term of Gaston Caperton, who had defeated Moore in his bid for reelection. Caperton presided over the unveiling of the upper portion of the dome with its newly applied gold leaf on June 20, 1990, West Virginia Day.

Although Tsitsilianos predicted the gilding would last fifty years, the gold developed black streaks, faded spots and chips within a few years and stayed that way for another decade. In 2002, Department of Administration officials estimated that about forty percent of the gilding had failed. Experts eventually determined that problems with the epoxy used in the gilding in 1990 caused it to fail and let dirt stick to the dome.

STRUCTURAL PROBLEMS

But the problems with the dome were much more than gold skin deep. "It was very bad," Tom Susman, who was acting secretary of administration during most of 2003 and half of 2004, said. "The eagle would move in the wind." He said he was told that someone in the 1970s came up with the idea of putting spikes around the base of the dome to let backed-up rainwater drain, but no one ever went back to fix the problem correctly, so rust developed. Susman said he and other Wise administration officials were so worried about the condition of the dome that they were afraid a strong wind might have knocked it off of the Capitol. Joe Manchin, who became governor in January 2005, and his administration secretary, Rob Ferguson, also shared that fear.

"The skeleton underneath was badly rusted," Ferguson said. "It was almost completely rusted through. We were told a hurricane-force wind would literally take it off."

Susman said someone came to him one time with a proposal to use a big helicopter to lift the lantern and eagle off of the dome and set them down next to the Capitol, apparently to facilitate repairs. He recalled, "I said, 'That's been up there for seventy years. When you pick it up, then the Capitol dome is going to expand. What happens then—would it crack or what?' I'm not an engineer, but that was kind of a bizarre day."

In October 2004, workers began putting up scaffolding and then wrapped the dome in a big sheath of white plastic. It made the Capitol look as though it was wearing a turban, although less-polite jokesters tended to compare it to a condom and quipped that it might promote "safe government." No matter what it was called, the covering was there for protection against the elements during a $5 million job to repair the dome and gild it again. State officials hoped to get it done right that time.

The plastic covering was the recommendation of Swanke Hayden Connell Architects, which the state again called on for help. The company determined that the surface of the dome had not been prepared properly in previous attempts to gild it. The plastic enclosure was intended to allow work to continue throughout the year, the company said, while maintaining "the precise temperature and humidity required for the gold leaf application. This seemingly simple tactic ensured the successful re-gilding of the dome and enabled the completion of the project nine months ahead of schedule." Under the firm's guidance, workers used a durable coating system to make

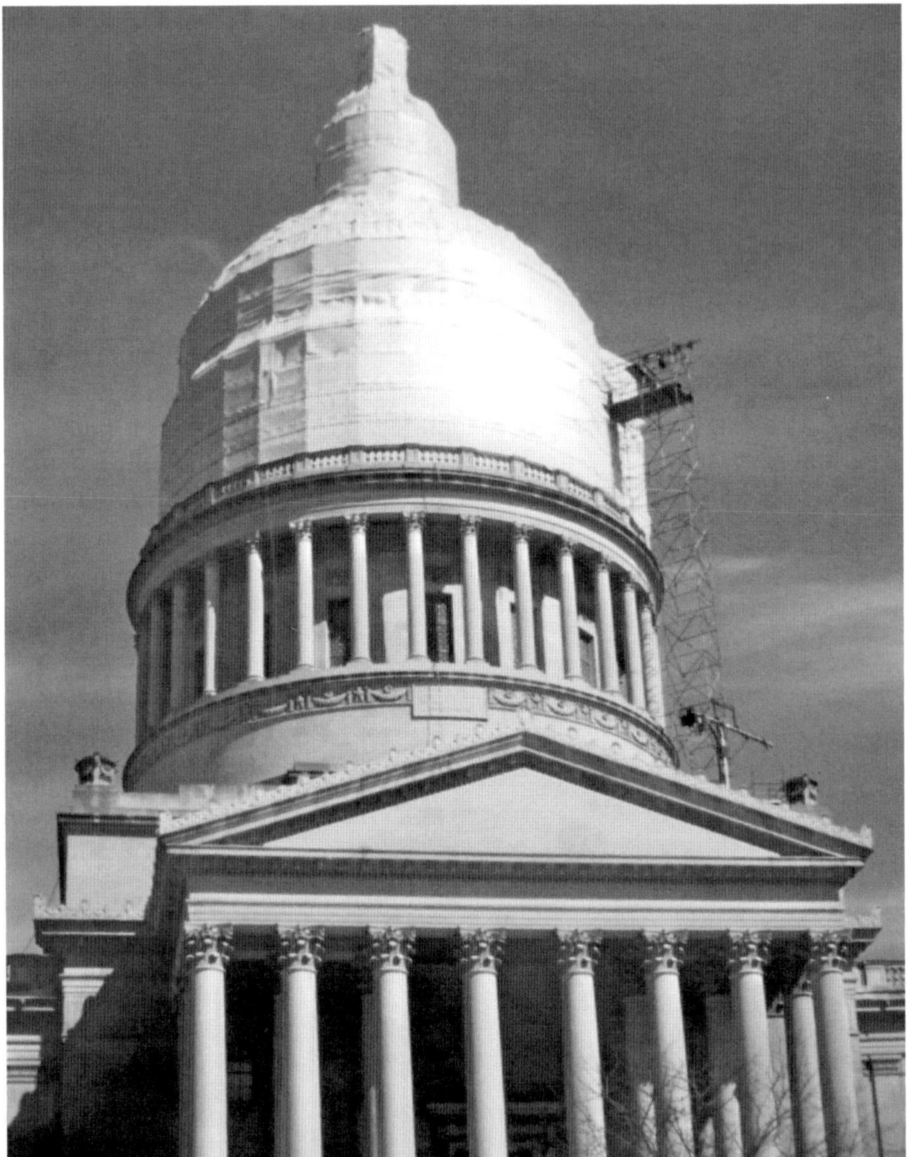

The dome of the Capitol was covered by plastic, as seen here on March 10, 2005, while workers repaired it and put new gold leaf on it. *Photo by Jim Wallace.*

sure the gold leaf would adhere properly. Swanke Hayden Connell Architects bragged that the project finished 10 percent under budget, which allowed additional exterior work to be done.

Work was already underway when Manchin became governor, but he decided that state residents should have a say in what the final result would be. He offered them the opportunity to vote online by computer or by phone on a toll-free line on two alternatives. One would be to cover the entire dome in gold as it had been since the gilding of 1988–90. The other would be to go back to Gilbert's original design of having gold leaf on the ribs and ornaments, as well as the lantern and eagle, while leaving the long panels around the ornaments a natural gray so those ornaments would stand out. About 80 percent of the more than twelve thousand votes tabulated favored the two-tone design, which Manchin revealed was his preference. He added that it would cost $214,500 less than applying gold leaf to the entire dome.

EAGLE ISSUES

Even the eagle at the top received close attention during that renovation. The eagle stands more than five feet tall with a three-foot-wide base on top of a ball, which is above a twenty-five-foot bronze spire atop the thirty-four-and-a-half-foot lantern at the apex of the dome.

When General Services workers inspected the eagle and the lantern in 2003, they found problems with the welds holding the lantern to the dome. David Pentz, director of the Division of General Services, blamed the problem on years of "deferred maintenance."

Later, John Wiseman of Wiseman Construction, the contractor on the repair job, discovered that the eagle had holes in it and needed new eyes. He told the *Charleston Daily Mail*, "Inside the eyes was a plastic material, kind of like you'd see on a bike reflector. And one of them was busted out." It was decided to give the eagle eyes made of West Virginia glass.

The refurbishing and gilding of the dome concluded in October 2005. A festival celebrated its new look. The project cost $5 million. In 1931, gilding the dome had cost less than $24,000. But the most recent gilding already has lasted longer in good condition than the previous efforts.

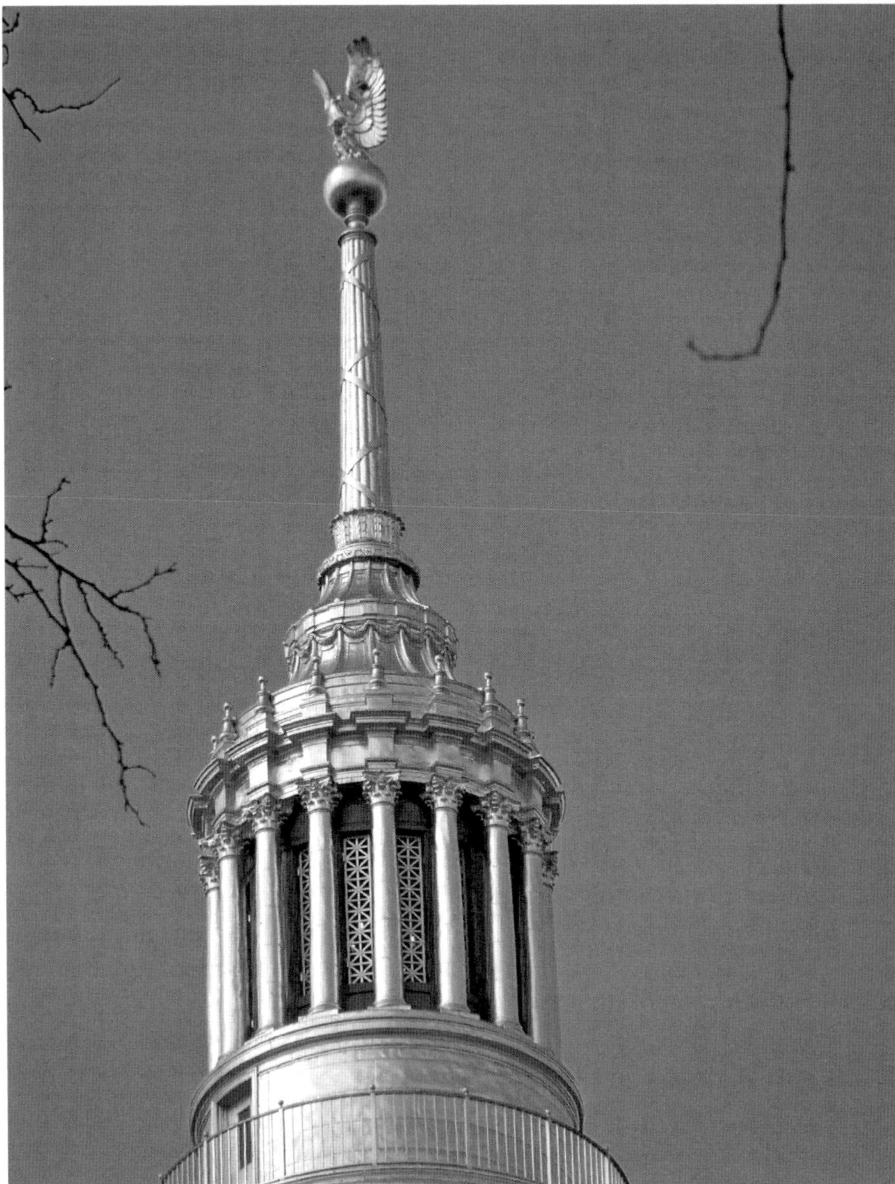

The eagle and lantern at the top of the dome were in bad shape before a renovation project that ended in 2005. *Photo by Jim Wallace.*

TROUBLE UNDER THE DOME

The outside of the dome was not alone in needing attention after decades of neglect. In 1996, the inside of the dome was repainted completely for the first time in sixty years. It was part of a $1.4 million project to return the inside of the dome to its 1932 appearance. For years, the color of the inner dome had ranged from dark blue to brown. It was returned to bright, but deep blue. Yellowed marble around the rotunda became white again.

The eight-foot-wide chandelier with 10,800 pieces of Czechoslovakian crystal and ninety-six light bulbs that normally hangs about 180 feet above the ground floor of the rotunda traditionally was lowered once every four years around the time each governor was inaugurated. That allowed it to be cleaned and repaired as well as displayed at a lower level for inaugural activities. However, after about 2000, it was lowered more often for special events such as conferences at the Capitol.

In November 2002, electrical problems developed. Only three light bulbs were reported to be working. The chandelier was lowered so the faulty bulbs could be replaced. That was the fourth time that year the chandelier had been lowered. But as it was being raised back up, five bulbs went out again. Apparently, the cable holding the fixture became crimped, causing an electrical short, which burned three of six strands in the cable. It also shocked an employee operating the crank at the top of the dome. At least one strand in the cable broke. That problem was much more serious than a loss of light. The fear was that, if the cable were weakened further, the chandelier could fall. Not only would the state have lost an irreplaceable chandelier but also the speculation was that its two-ton weight would have caused it to crash through the marble of the ground floor and into the basement cafeteria below with shards of crystal flying in all directions. Jim Burgess, deputy director of General Services, said it was possible that without a floor to support the beams that hold up the upper part of the rotunda, the entire middle section of the Capitol might have collapsed.

Workers initially raised the chandelier high enough—about fifty to sixty feet—to relax the tension on the damaged cable. That brought it several feet higher than the second floor well of the rotunda. Engineers then attached additional support cables to make the chandelier more secure.

That December, workers used scaffolding to lower the chandelier carefully to the floor of the rotunda, where electricians rewired it and installed a new cable, as well as a new motor and pulley system. The old light bulbs were replaced with longer-lasting bulbs. The cost was $35,000,

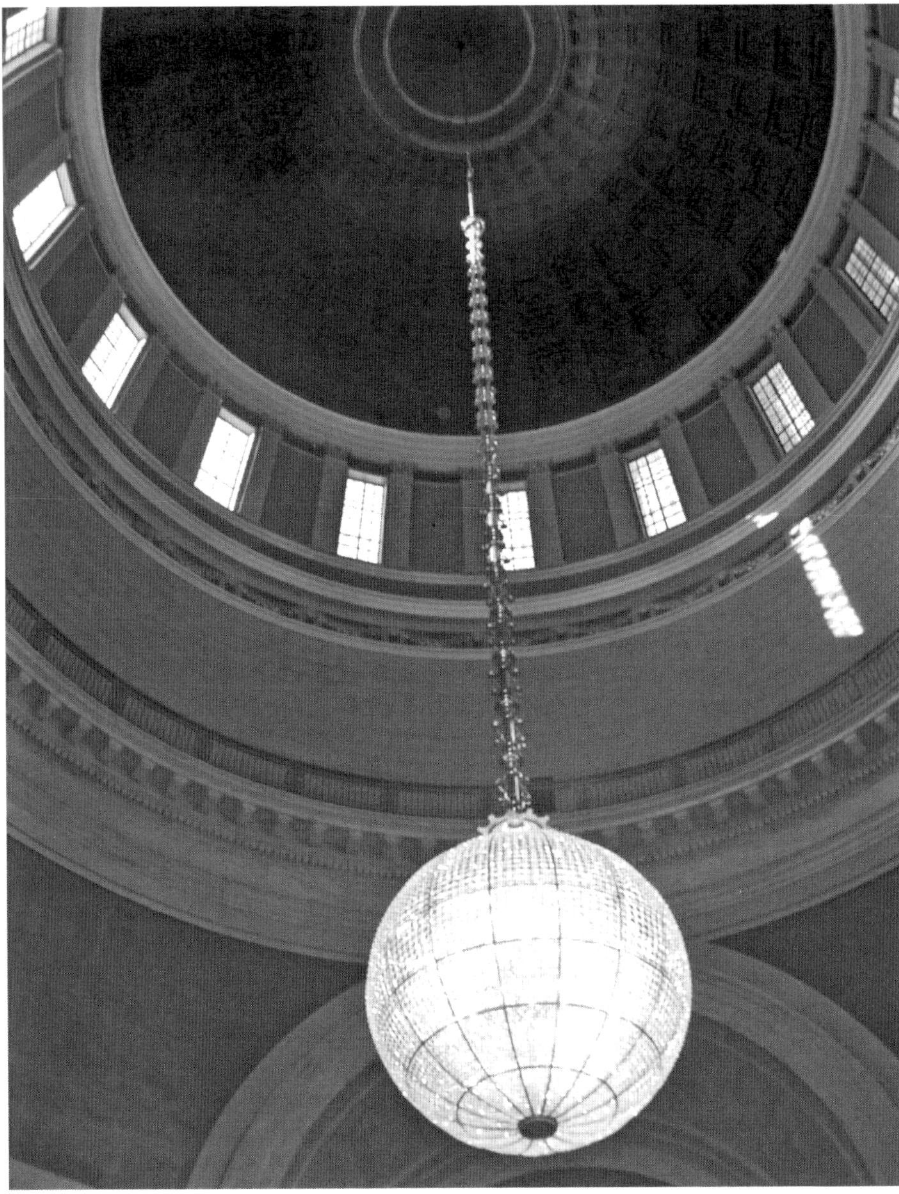

In 2002 and 2003, state officials were afraid the chandelier hanging in the rotunda might fall, crash through the marble floor and perhaps cause the central section of the Capitol's main unit to fall in. *Photo by Jim Wallace.*

but losing a seventy-year-old, imported chandelier of a type that was no longer being made would have been much costlier. It was restored to its normal position high in the rotunda in time for the regular legislative session in January 2003.

The problem seemed to be resolved, at least until September 2003, when the chandelier was lowered while the Capitol hosted a Southern Governors' Association reception. When workers raised the chandelier after that event, the cable snagged and tore partially. Officials evacuated the basement cafeteria and blocked off the rotunda floor just in case the chandelier would fall. As a precaution, workers spent what was reported to be about three hours to lower the chandelier slowly to the floor. But Tom Susman, the administration secretary at the time, recalled that it seemed "like the longest eight hours of my life." The repair crew determined that one of the cable's four securing clamps slipped, so they replaced it and added a fifth clamp for extra security. The chandelier went back up that October.

A few years later, when Rob Ferguson was in charge of the Department of Administration, the concerns were that anchors holding the chandeliers hanging in the House and Senate chambers were weakening. He said he was especially concerned that the House chandelier might fall. "As a result of that, we have recurring, scheduled maintenance on all those things now," Ferguson said. "They're on a routine calendar schedule."

Fortunately, the chandeliers did not fall. Nor did the dome ever get blown off of the building, but parts of the Capitol have fallen at times. For example, in 1987, a three-hundred-pound chunk of stone fell from the north portico about one hundred feet to the lawn below. The problem was blamed on the freezing and thawing of water that seeped between the stone and the rest of the building. About the same time, a forty-eight-foot crack developed in an outside wall from the base of the south portico entrance to the ceiling. An expert determined that metal straps used to anchor the limestone blocks had rusted away. Those problems were repaired, but similar problems were found more than a decade later.

WEAKNESS IN THE WALLS

Among the most serious problems discovered were those with the parapet walls that run along the edges of the Capitol roofs. As early as 2001, someone noticed that one of those walls had been moving and cracking. Once again, the blame was placed on water that had been seeping into cracks and then freezing and thawing over the years. That was causing walls to crack and water to leak into the building.

By May 2002, administration officials warned legislators to be prepared for extensive and expensive repairs. Jim Burgess, deputy director of the General Services Division, said there were so many cracks along the parapet wall allowing water to get in that he was afraid big sections of wall could eventually fall. Repairing just the corner over the offices of the governor and the Senate president would take several months and cost $200,000, but he said all of the big stones needed to be pulled out and reinstalled with new caulking.

"There's an enormous amount of caulking failure," Burgess said. "The more water that gets in that, the more it's going to move." As he pointed to a section of stone above the House of Delegates chamber with at least an inch of separation from the one adjacent to it, he said, "The terra cotta walls are like honeycombs; the water goes anywhere." During the legislative session earlier that year, one delegate complained that dust had fallen onto members' desks from arches overhead that had been damaged by water, and it was easy for visitors in the House galleries to see flaking paint on those arches. The problems even prompted Senate President Earl Ray Tomblin to go up on the Capitol roof that spring to inspect the problems himself.

Also that spring, experts told the legislature many more repairs needed to be made, including the replacement of five of the six boilers that heated the building, renovation of the antiquated restrooms, replacement of energy-inefficient windows and repair or replacement of big brass doors, along with repairs and new gilding for the dome. That July, the legislature received the estimate for making all of the repairs: $87 million. The repair of the parapet wall, at a cost of $14.5 million, was deemed to be the most urgent.

The repairs could not be made soon enough, because in December 2003, a section of ceiling about ten feet by ten feet in a third-floor conference room collapsed. Fortunately, the room was empty at the time. Earlier that year, chunks of concrete fell from the parking garage along California Avenue known as Building 2. Even though it had been designed by Cass Gilbert Jr., the administration tore it down that fall.

In their 2004 regular session, legislators voted to spend more than $24 million over a couple of years to get started on the many repairs: $15.9 million the first year and $8.5 the following year. By that spring, state officials also faced the need to replace elevators in Buildings 3, 5 and 6, as well as renovate those in the main Capitol building. On May 25, 2004, all four of the elevators in Building 3, which has eight floors, broke down, but that was just the most serious of a long series of elevator malfunctions in that and the other buildings.

MORE PROBLEMS

Although the Wise administration began the process of catching up on repairs that were needed after years of deferred maintenance, plenty of work was left for the Manchin administration when it began in 2005, and even for the administration of Earl Ray Tomblin after he took over as governor in 2010. "The entire Capitol needed a new roof," Rob Ferguson, who was administration secretary from January 2005 until February 2012, said. "It was leaking terribly. Our master electrical systems and feeds to the Capitol were antiques and in danger of not only power failures but fires. We literally spent several million dollars replacing electrical feeds. We referred to it as the Frankenstein monster in the basement. There were these transformers in the basement that were literally from the '30s and '40s."

If the electrical problems had not been fixed, the Capitol could have had a catastrophic power failure that could have lasted for more than just days, he said. Ferguson said his own office on the ground floor was damaged by plumbing problems and water leaks that sometimes came all the way from the roof. When he had workers repair the problems, they removed three sets of lowered ceilings that had been installed from the 1950s through the 1980s and restored the original high ceilings.

While attending to long-needed repairs, Ferguson also made other interesting discoveries. For example, he said there are a couple of landings of about one thousand square feet near the stairwell in the dome. Soon after he came into office, he went up there and found "couches, some chairs and a distinct smell of cigar smoke imbedded everywhere, so I think it had become kind of a lounge."

Sometimes, the work that needed to be done on the Capitol was to undo features that had been added even though they did not fit with Gilbert's intent. For example, for more than two decades, the east wing of the Capitol had a mezzanine. Agriculture Commissioner Gus Douglass, who had his offices in that part of the Capitol at the time, had the mezzanine built in 1971 despite complaints by some people who objected to altering Gilbert's design.

It provided about 2,200 square feet of office space, but by July 1990, an architect contracted by the state determined the mezzanine had deteriorated so much that it was hazardous, because its floor, which was then the ceiling for ground-floor offices, had sagged. By then, the agriculture commissioner's office was no longer using the mezzanine because the department had moved most of its operations to facilities at Guthrie, north of Charleston. In 1992, the mezzanine was removed.

Also in 1992, state officials realized that planters that had been installed in the middle of five sidewalks leading up to the Capitol were not part of Gilbert's design and should be removed. The planters were deteriorating at the time, so instead of spending as much as $9,000 to replace them, the Capitol Building Commission decided to remove them and put gray paving stones in their place. It was another case in which following what Gilbert had planned was cheaper than deviating from his design. For workers who had become accustomed to sitting on the sides of the planters during breaks, the administration installed stone benches along the sides of the walks.

Ceilings and Furniture

That year, 1992, turned out to be quite a year for restoring the Capitol to Gilbert's vision. Another such effort that year involved murals on first-floor ceilings in the west and east wings. Gilbert had wanted murals to be painted on ceilings and walls all around the building. "Mural decorations of an adequate character should embellish the rotunda and the house and senate, and in the reception rooms and corridors surrounding the house and senate chambers there should be reasonable modest but adequate decorative treatment," he wrote in his letter to Governor Conley. Yet most of those ceilings and walls remained blank. Only the first-floor ceiling murals in the wings are believed to have been painted under Gilbert's direction during construction of the Capitol. Thus, they serve as isolated indications of what the rest of the building might have come to look like. The murals depict angelic women wearing flowing dresses and carrying leafy branches, flowers and, in one case, a sphere.

But by 1992, the murals' beauty had faded quite a bit. In some spots, paint had flaked off, but most of the damage was blamed on accumulated resin from more than six decades of cigarette smoke. (Protecting the Capitol is one reason why smoking has been prohibited in most of the building in

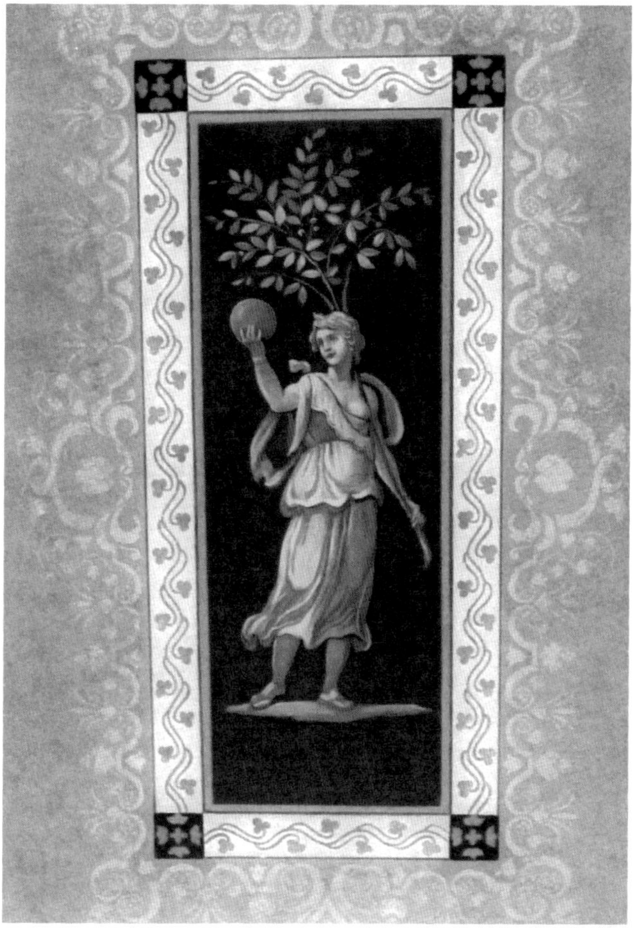

Artwork on the first-floor ceiling of the west wing is an indication of what kind of murals Cass Gilbert wanted throughout the Capitol. *Photo by Jim Wallace.*

recent years, although some stubborn legislators have been known to ignore that ban while in their offices.) The murals in the west wing were in worse shape than those in the east wing. To put the murals back close to their original condition, state officials brought in two art restoration experts, one from Indiana and one from Arizona, to fix them. They used solvents to clean the grime off of the original paint where possible. Where paint was missing, they blended new paint to match the colors and texture of the original.

Paint on murals was not the only thing from Gilbert's work that turned up missing over the years. So did furniture that had been designed or selected by him. It became a big issue for several legislators and others in the mid-1980s when they learned that some officeholders had been allowed to take furniture with them when they left office. Governor Clarence Meadows, who served from 1945 to 1949, was said to have been the first to do that. Reportedly, other officeholders had some furniture declared surplus property, which allowed them to purchase it very cheaply.

Darrell McGraw confirmed some of those reports in 1985, when he was a Supreme Court justice. He told the *Charleston Gazette* that, soon after he was elected to the court in 1976, he learned that many of the Capitol's original pieces of furniture had been stowed away in a basement room and in a fourth-floor room nicknamed "the boneyard." McGraw said former Justice Sam Harshbarger and Jack Bowman, a former court administrator, joined him in rescuing some of that furniture. By doing so, McGraw acquired a desk, two tables, a couch, two brass spittoons, a coat tree and a wastebasket, which he believed all dated back to the Capitol's early days. That *Gazette* article called the Supreme Court chamber "the largest single-room depository of original furnishings anywhere in the Capitol." It said the justices' chairs were original as were forty-four other refurbished chairs and four flag holders, two of which had been restored and two that were awaiting restoration.

Although some people doubted that it would have been the responsibility of the architect to choose or design furniture for the building, such doubts were put to rest by checking a copy of the official souvenir program from the Capitol's dedication in 1932. "The furniture, floor coverings and draperies in West Virginia's beautiful Capitol Building were furnished and installed by the George P. Reinhard Co. under the direction of Cass Gilbert Inc.," an advertisement from the firm stated. "Architecture, interior decoration and the designing and construction of furniture are closely related fields." Like Gilbert's company, Reinhard also was based in New York City.

But not all of the original furniture installed in the Capitol came from Reinhard. In 2003, when the hand-carved mahogany desks in the House of Delegates chamber were restored, the workers found "Bentley & Gerwig Furniture Company" stamped on the bottom of each drawer. That company operated for decades in the late 1800s and early 1900s in Parkersburg.

Renewed Chambers

The House and Senate both have renovated their chambers and meeting rooms at times. Modest but significant additions came when they added sound systems. The House installed a $10,000 speaker system with a microphone at each member's desk, as well as a system for recording proceedings on magnetic tape, in 1951. But it took until 1960 for the Senate to install a similar system with a microphone for each member, although by then, it had used floor microphones set up near the majority and minority leaders for five years. Unlike the House, the Senate did not begin recording its proceedings right away. Since then, speaker systems, electronic tally boards for votes and other technology have been updated several times, including the addition of computers in recent years.

However, other renovations in the legislative chambers sometimes have sparked criticism from people who worried that such changes were deviating from Gilbert's design or too expensive or both. In the mid-1980s, the Senate came under criticism for work done at costs that would pale in comparison to later projects. In 1984, it was for spending $167,000 to fix up the Senate Judiciary Committee's meeting room on the second floor of the west wing. One year later, it was for spending $16,500 on custom-made walnut furniture in the Senate chamber, but it was not just to provide such ordinary furniture as tables and chairs. It was for a structure that would allow the assistant clerk, two assistant journal editors, a sound operator, two shorthand reporters and a recording operator to sit together in front of the president's podium. Previously, the recording operator had to work from the basement, the two employees who took shorthand were seated at separate desks on the Senate floor and the others sat at a long bench. The new structure also accommodated a new computer terminal and a computer operator. To make room for all that, seating for news reporters was moved to the back of the chamber.

A decade later, the House spent $774,000 for more extensive renovations to its chamber, which invited stronger criticism, especially because the work originally was estimated to cost about $400,000. The renovations, which began in the spring of 1995 and concluded in the fall of that year, included new carpeting, drapes, paint and wiring, as well as a new sound system and a new electronic voting system. In addition, the walls and ceilings were re-plastered, and a new conference room was built behind the chamber. Also, a permanent ramp for wheelchairs replaced temporary ramps, and walnut pews replaced theater-style seats in the galleries. (The Senate still has the old gallery seats, which have racks underneath to hold the fedoras that men tended to wear in the early and middle years of the twentieth century.) Several old, wooden phone booths that stood in the room behind the speaker's podium were removed. The delegates' desks and chairs were refurbished but not restored to the extent they were in 2003. Although the House received some renovations in 1982, the 1995 project was the most complete refurbishing the chamber had received since it went into use in 1932.

Several delegates complained that they never had a chance to have a say in the project before it was well underway, but Speaker Chuck Chambers said the decision was his to make as the presiding officer of the House.

AROUND THE GROUNDS

The grounds around the Capitol also have undergone many changes over the years, sometimes to carry out Gilbert's plans and sometimes to deviate from them. In his 1932 letter to Governor Conley, Gilbert wrote that "terraces, steps, and approaches" were all essential to the Capitol's design.

"I mention these factors at this time as indicating that this phase of the project is not an additional one but merely carries to completion that which was originally contemplated," he wrote. Without such landscaping features, he said, the Capitol would be as incomplete "as though the buildings were without cornices or porticos." Gilbert emphasized that it was not unusual to construct terraces around public buildings.

"This work of the development of the grounds should not be a matter of casual action of incidental grading and planting, but should be carefully and seriously planned by the architect," he wrote. But of course, it was easier for Gilbert to make such a plea than for state officials to grant his wishes in the depths of the Great Depression. Landscaping around the Capitol was modest in its early years.

In 1939 and 1940, Governor Homer Holt and others worked closely with Cass Gilbert Jr. on improving the riverbank, including the building of a retaining wall, in front of the Capitol. They cooperated on that project with the City of Charleston, which was enlarging what had been Kanawha Street and transforming it into Kanawha Boulevard.

Holt seemed to be as pleased with the younger Gilbert's work as his predecessors had been with that of the older Gilbert. In a July 1940 letter to the son, the governor wrote: "Our people are quite generally most favorably impressed by this river bank development and those who have, perhaps, a better and more complete appreciation of art are indeed enthusiastic about it, as I am, of course."

In the landscaping plans that Cass Gilbert Sr. drew up, he wanted a fountain to be built in the courtyard on the north side of the building between the two wings. That project had to wait until after World War II. Work began in 1946 and was completed in 1947. Cars were allowed to park

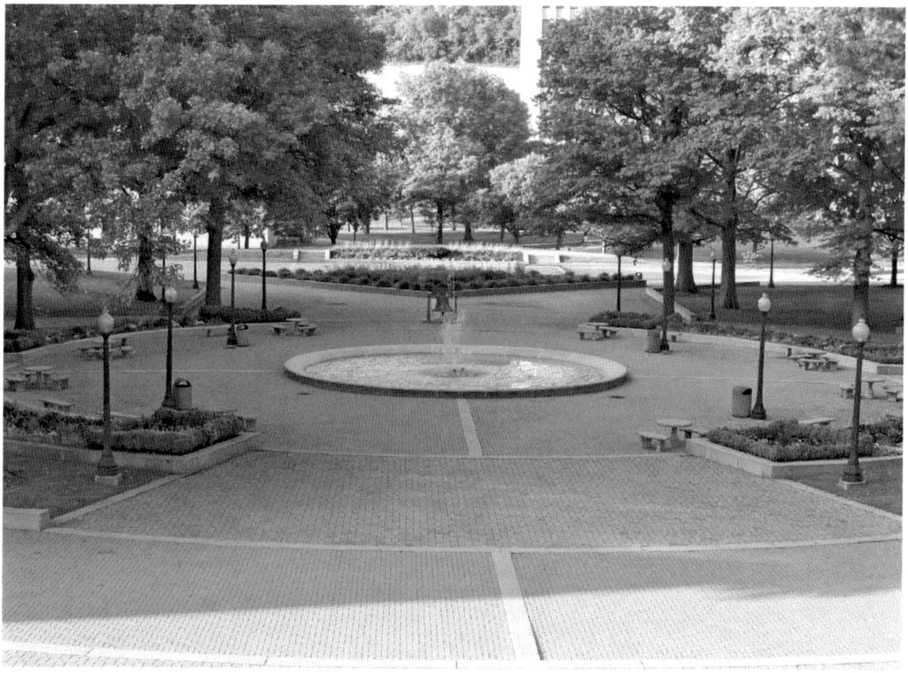

The fountain in the Capitol Circle was part of Cass Gilbert's original design, but it was not built until a dozen years after his death. *Photo by Jim Wallace.*

around the fountain in the Capitol Circle for the next four decades. Although many legislators prized the fifty-five parking spaces around the fountain for their convenience, those spaces were eliminated when the portion of Washington Street that went through the Capitol Complex was closed in 1988. The impetus for that change was not so much Gilbert's vision but that of Governor Arch Moore, who wanted a "campus setting" with less asphalt and more greenery for the Capitol Complex. Removal of the cars made room for large flowerbeds, more trees and grass. The addition of several new sidewalks also made the grounds friendlier to pedestrians. A guardhouse that had stood by the circle was moved to the corner of Greenbrier and Washington Streets.

"One of the best moves they made was when they closed the circle for parking," Tom Susman, a former legislator and former administrator secretary, said. "I was in the House, and we'd park in the circle. It was awful. We had this beautiful Capitol, and we had these cars up on the sidewalk. It's really nice now. That made it a campus."

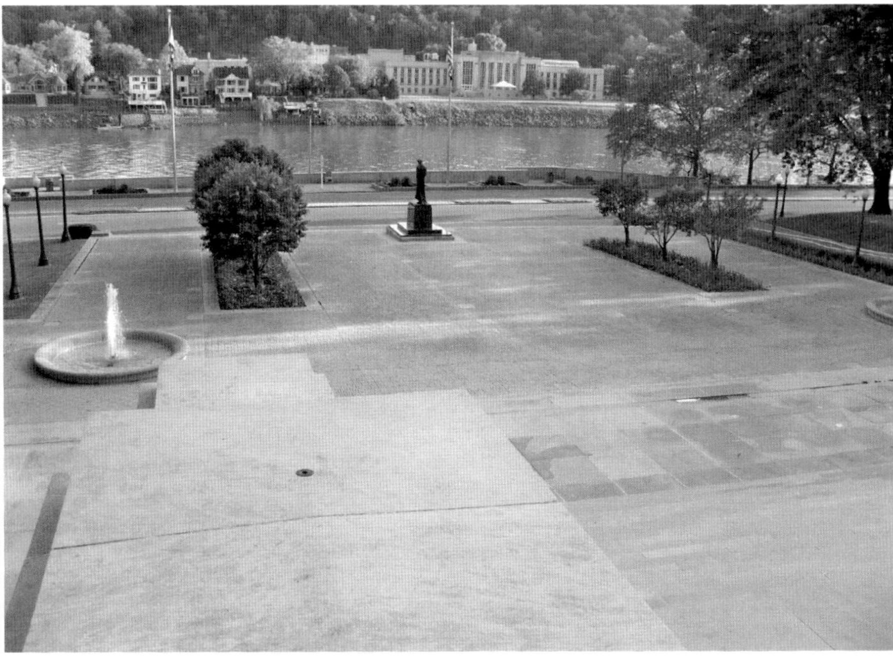

The plaza in front of the steps on the south side of the Capitol was expanded in 1996 to make it more like what Gilbert had envisioned. *Photo by Jim Wallace.*

Another feature of landscaping designed by Cass Gilbert Sr. took more than six decades to be implemented. He had designed a much bigger plaza on the south side of the Capitol, the side nearest the Kanawha River, than was built in the 1930s. In 1996, the Caperton administration, with help from Charleston architect Paul Marshall and about $200,000 provided by the legislature, put in two round water fountains, each smaller than the fountain on the north side, at the base of the Capitol steps. The plaza was expanded by about twenty feet on each side so that it was equal to the width of the steps. The project also included a wheelchair-accessible ramp.

During the winter of 2010, the Capitol Complex lost a large, oval fountain that had stood for four decades in front of Buildings 5, 6 and 7, but no one seemed to mourn its absence. It had twelve jets of water in the center and a dozen more around the perimeter. It was large enough to have been compared to Cleopatra's barge, and many people considered it not very attractive. Norman Fagan, who was executive director of the West Virginia Arts and Humanities Council when the fountain was built in 1970, called it "the Jolly Green Giant's bidet." By the time it was removed, it had not worked right for years. "The plumbing was really bad on it," Rob Ferguson, who was administration secretary when the fountain was removed, said. "The thing hadn't been maintained in years. It was leaking terribly. It was just a money pit."

Another problem was that the inside wall was as much fifteen feet high, which was considered dangerous for anyone who might climb on it. Workers replaced the fountain with green space, along with dozens of wooden tables, chairs and benches.

TOWARD A SAFER CAMPUS

Many of the changes made to the Capitol Complex in the twenty-first century have been security enhancements. Concern about security escalated after September 11, 2001, when terrorist-hijacked planes flew into the World Trade Center towers in New York City and the Pentagon just outside Washington, D.C., and another plane apparently heading for Washington crashed instead in a Pennsylvania field. Even the West Virginia Capitol was evacuated that day when officials became suspicious about a plane that seemed to be heading for Charleston.

But efforts to improve security actually began a few years earlier when, in 1998, Governor Underwood persuaded the legislature during a special session to create the Division of Protective Services. Until then, the Division of General Services contracted with a private company to provide security guards for the complex. It took until 1999 for legislators to provide funding for the new agency, which soon set up a centralized mailroom with an X-ray machine to check suspicious packages. In December 1999, the division began setting up closed-circuit security cameras around the campus at a cost of $359,000.

In 2001, Governor Bob Wise worked with the legislature in a special session to appropriate $819,000 for more security measures. The agency soon began a project to control public access to buildings around the complex with the notable exceptions of the Capitol and the Culture Center. About half of that money was spent on putting electronic locks on building doors that employees could use swipe cards to open. Members of the public had to pass through new metal detectors in three locations to get into those buildings. One was set up at Building 3. Another was installed at Building 7 to serve not only that building but also Buildings 5 and 6, which are connected to it.

The third was placed in Building 15, where the Division of Purchasing is located, one block east of the Capitol.

The state also bought metal detectors for the main Capitol building but abandoned plans to install them. Plans were to limit public access to just three or four entrances, instead of nineteen, with metal detectors and X-ray scanners, but legislators and other officials balked at the cost of having guards staff those checkpoints at least twelve hours a day. In 2004, a Protective Services official estimated the agency would need to hire at least eighteen more officers to do that. Many legislators also did not like the idea of restricting public access to the Capitol. But while the proposal to limit access to the building was still being considered, it led to the construction of a big ramp for wheelchair access on the east side of the Capitol. The Supreme Court demanded that people should be able to get to the court chamber without having to go through the whole building, and the only way to accommodate that for those in wheelchairs, if access had been limited, was to put a ramp on that side.

In 2005, Protective Services spent almost $304,000 and moved its command center from a small, former storage room into a larger room in the Capitol basement. It featured a wall full of monitors for watching more than two hundred security cameras around the complex, both inside buildings and outside.

Another project costing more than $449,000 began in 2008, partly in response to two incidents the prior year in which impaired drivers brought vehicles onto the Capitol grounds. One of them caused damage to the Veterans Memorial estimated at $500,000. The state erected metal gates at thirteen entrances to the Capitol Complex to keep unauthorized vehicles out during nonbusiness hours and installed more security cameras.

In 2009, security officials came up with a plan to put up a six-foot-tall fence of black wrought iron and columns made of concrete and bricks, as well as Victorian-style lanterns, around 960 feet of perimeter of the complex, including in front of the Governor's Mansion and Holly Grove. But they withdrew that plan in the face of public opposition. The following year, the state spent $346,000 for more security measures, including the installation of four sets of stainless-steel hydraulic bollards that retract into the ground when authorized vehicles need to get through but otherwise block vehicular traffic. Those bollards attracted little attention, but strong opposition erupted in 2011 after the Department of Administration—without getting approval from the Capitol Building Commission—had a contractor install fifty-eight dome-shaped concrete bollards, thirty-two inches tall and thirty inches wide, to serve as vehicular barriers around the campus. Within weeks, the bollards, which weighed 1,100 pounds each, were removed. Fortunately for the state, the National Guard found a use for them. Another part of that year's $459,000 worth of security measures was the construction of a ninety-six-foot retaining wall of concrete and limestone along Piedmont Road west of the parking garage.

Although the abandoned plans for a wrought-iron fence and concrete bollards stirred up many protests, many security measures have gone almost unnoticed because they used landscaping, or "environmental design," to make vehicular access to the campus more difficult. They include the formation of small mounds, often topped by flowers and other plants, and the placement of bushes, concrete planters and marble benches to make it difficult for any vehicle to get very far if it does intrude onto the grounds of the Capitol.

But Rob Ferguson, who served as administration secretary for seven years until early 2012, said the landscaping security measures were not meant to be permanent solutions. "Those were expedient fixes meant to be temporary only, because if someone wants to do us harm, those are easily bypassed," he said. "But it was designed as a stopgap measure until we really figured out what the plan was going to be."

Ferguson said the National Guard had the assignment to devise further security measures, but by the time he left office, there was "an architectural plan to put low-rise walls—something along the lines of eighteen to twenty-four inches to prevent cars from going on campus—trying to make it blend into the campus landscape."

PLANNING AND FUNDING

When the concrete bollards were removed in 2011, it was the result of an order by the Capitol Building Commission, which the Department of Administration had not consulted before installing the bollards. That Capitol Building Commission was not the agency by the same name that oversaw planning and construction of the Capitol in the 1920s and 1930s. That commission was disbanded shortly after the construction was completed. But in 1976, the legislature created a new Capitol Building Commission in response to problems caused by changes made by agencies that did not follow Cass Gilbert's designs. Legislators let the commission be terminated in 1986, but they reestablished it again in 1990. It consists of five voting members: the commissioner of the

Division of Culture and History, one architect, one engineer and two members from the public at large. The secretary of the Department of Administration serves as a nonvoting member. The commissioner of culture and history is the chairperson. The commission has the authority to approve or reject all plans for substantial physical changes inside or outside of buildings on the Capitol Complex. The degree to which the commission has exerted such authority has varied over the years. For example, Susman said the Wise administration, which was in office from 2001 until 2005, largely ignored the commission, but it has been more active since then.

For funding for modifications and repairs around the Capitol Complex, both Susman and Ferguson give much credit to Oshel Craigo and Earl Ray Tomblin, who, as leaders of the Senate Finance Committee in the mid-1990s, crafted legislation to set aside a portion of video lottery revenues first for completion of the Veterans Memorial and then for maintenance of other monuments and features around the grounds. "It's special revenue that's earmarked for what it's supposed to be spent for," Craigo said. "So they don't have to go back year in and year out to ask for funds to do it with."

Prior to that, Susman said, it was difficult to get legislators to set aside enough money to keep up with maintenance and repairs around the Capitol Complex. In 2004, the legislature changed the allocation from the lottery funds to provide money not only for the upkeep of monuments and other features on the Capitol grounds but also for any repairs and maintenance needed inside or outside of the Capitol and its related buildings. At that time, it provided about $5 million a year, but it has grown to be $8 million to $10 million in recent years. Ferguson said, "We wouldn't have been able to accomplish any of the things we accomplished without that fund. That is the aorta of cash flow for General Services."

Another action taken early in the Wise administration has allowed the state to understand better exactly what Gilbert had intended for the Capitol. In May 2001, the Division of Culture and History successfully bid $12,925 in an online auction to acquire Gilbert's original drawings and other documents about the Capitol. The collection also included the sketches that Cass Gilbert Jr. made for Building 3.

But in June 2012, Ferguson said what the Capitol Complex needs is not just the Gilberts' plans from the past but also better plans for the future, some that would survive changes of governors, cabinet secretaries and legislators. "We've never really had—that we could find—a holistic approach for design of the Capitol campus," he said. "It's always kind of been a hodge-podge."

CHAPTER 10

THE HOUSE OF STATE

The view that many people get of the West Virginia Capitol is quick and fleeting as they drive through Charleston on Interstate 77/64. They likely are unaware of political battles that have been fought, the ceremonies that have been held or the people great and minor who have toiled there. But certainly it should be apparent that this majestic building with its golden dome makes a statement that West Virginia and its citizens matter in the course of human events.

Cass Gilbert did not foresee the freeway that would cut through the hillside just north of the Capitol, but he did offer a clear vision of what the Capitol should be:

> *Public buildings, and especially the State Capitol, constitute the best evidence of the character of material, success and solidity, culture and civilization of a state. This has always been so. Great statesmen and rulers throughout the world from most ancient times, whether of monarchies, empires or republics, have signalized their existence by the character of their buildings. This is not an argument for extravagance; it is an argument for something totally different—namely, for economy in the preservation of the things the State has paid for, and it is not based upon the illusion of glory of magnificence. It is a simple business fact that a merchant in showing his goods displays them in his windows and on his counters in such a manner as to evidence their quality. It is in that sense a business proposition that the building for the State should evidence the substantial*

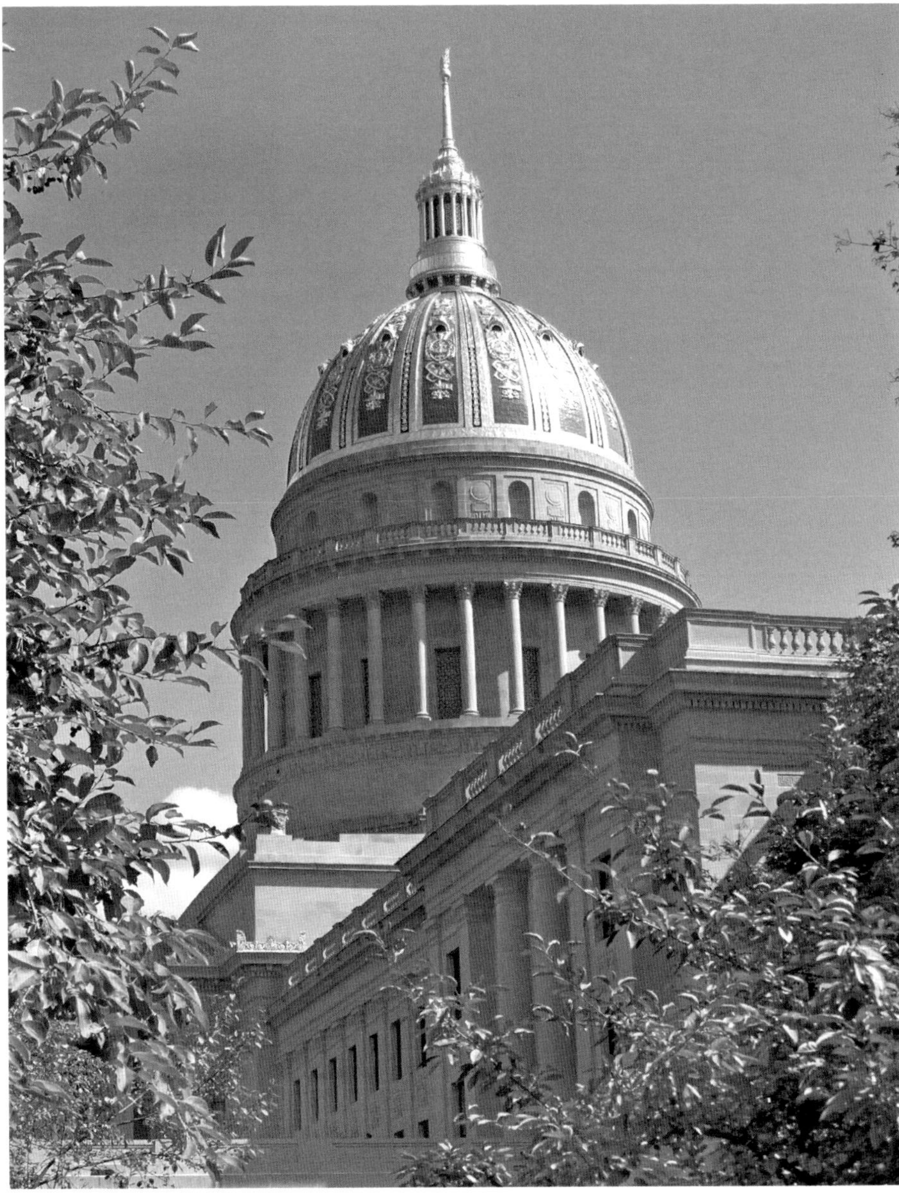

West Virginia's Capitol now sits along the Kanawha River on Charleston's East End, but the seat of state government has not always been located there. *Photo by Jim Wallace.*

> *character and civilization of the State, because (if for no other reason) it inspires confidence in the State on the part of both its own people and of all who visit it. Lavish expenditure and extravagance are to be deplored and avoided; they should have no part in such structures. The expenditure of a people's money is a public trust, and unwise expenditure is just the reverse of the impression that should be conveyed.*

As Gilbert asserted, the Capitol is a representation of the people of the state: people who have revered their statehouse and yet often neglected it; people who delight in the glitter of the gold dome but are reluctant to spend too much on it; people who are proud to be West Virginians while also quick to criticize their leaders.

The facts, figures and stories of this book are but a hint of what can be found in and around the Capitol: all the curves and corners, columns and carvings created by architects and artisans, as well as the narratives of those who have turned the wheels of government within its chambers, hallways and meeting rooms. It is a shame that so many travelers get nothing more than a glimpse of limestone and gold leaf, but even those who have spent decades on its campus have yet to discover all that can be found at this house of state.

Appendix

Capitol Chronology

1815—Daniel Ruffner built Holly Grove mansion on the grounds of what later became the Capitol Complex.

1861—April 17: Delegates of the Richmond Convention approved an ordinance of secession, leading to the withdrawal of Virginia from the Union.

1861—May 13: The First Wheeling Convention, which set the stage for the creation of West Virginia, began.

1861—June 13: At the first session of the Second Wheeling Convention, John Carlile presented "A Declaration of the People of Virginia," which called for the reorganization of the government of Virginia on the grounds that, because of Virginia's decision to secede from the United States, all state government offices had been vacated.

1861—June 20: Francis Pierpont became governor of the "reorganized" state of Virginia.

1861—October 24: A referendum approved creation of a new state.

1862—July 14: The United States Senate approved statehood for West Virginia by a vote of 23–17.

1862—December 31: President Abraham Lincoln signed the West Virginia statehood bill.

1863—June 20: West Virginia became the thirty-fifth state.

1869—January: Charleston offered $50,000 to build new Capitol.

1870—March 28: Governor William Stevenson and other state officials boarded the steamboat *Mountain Boy* to move capital from Wheeling to Charleston.

1870—March 30: State officials and records arrived in Charleston.

1870—April 1: Charleston officially became West Virginia's capital.

1870—December 20: State agencies moved into the first Charleston Capitol.

1875—February 20: The legislature voted to move the capital back to Wheeling.

1875—March 30: Charleston citizens filed suit in attempt to prevent capital from moving.

1875—May 21: Governor John Jacob and several other state officials left Charleston for Wheeling, aboard the steamer *Emma Graham*.

1875—May 23: State leaders arrived in Wheeling but without state records.

1875—September 13: West Virginia Supreme Court ruled in favor of capital's return to Wheeling

1875—September 22: A steamer and two barges departed Charleston to take state records to Wheeling.

1876—December 4: New Capitol in Wheeling became ready for use.

1877—August 7: West Virginians voted to make Charleston the state's permanent capital over Clarksburg and Martinsburg.

1885—May 1: Charleston officially became the capital again.

1885—May 3: State officials and records returned to Charleston.

1887—New Capitol, the second in Charleston, became fully ready for use.

1890—West Virginia Historical and Antiquarian Society was organized and set up display of artifacts, the beginning of the State Museum.

1893—State bought house at 153 Capitol Street to serve as first Governor's Mansion.

1894—April 3: Governor William MacCorkle announced the opening of the West Virginia State Museum in the Capitol.

1899—State officials planned to build the Capitol Annex.

1903—Capitol Annex was completed.

1905—Legislature passed act to legally incorporate artifacts from the West Virginia Historical and Antiquarian Society into the State Museum.

1910—*Stonewall Jackson* statue was dedicated on grounds of Capitol in downtown Charleston.

1912—*Mountaineer Soldier* statue was dedicated on grounds of Capitol in downtown Charleston.

1921—January 3: Fire destroyed the Capitol in downtown Charleston.

1921—January 14: State officials decided to build the temporary "Pasteboard Capitol."

1921—January 21: West Virginia Senate voted 20–10 in favor of a resolution to build a new permanent Capitol in Charleston.

1921—July 7: The state paid $64,270 for three parcels in Charleston's East End for new Governor's Mansion.

1921—July 21: Capitol Building Commission chose Cass Gilbert to be architect for new Capitol.

1921—December: Capitol Building Commission chose the Duffy Street site in Charleston's East End for the new Capitol.

1923—John Eichleay Jr. Company of Pittsburgh moved about fifty houses away from the site for the new Capitol, including moving a dozen of them across the river on barges.

1923—December 22: The state awarded contracts for construction of the Capitol's west wing with the George A. Fuller Company getting the general construction contract.

1924—January 7: Groundbreaking ceremony for west wing was held.

1924—Construction of new Governor's Mansion began with the Wallace Knight Construction Company the main contractor.

1924—May 1: Cornerstone was laid for west wing.

1925—Construction of new Governor's Mansion was completed.

1925—Construction of west wing finished.

1926—July: James Baird Company began construction of east wing.

1926—Garage with servants' quarters on top was built next to Governor's Mansion.

1926—November 30: Cornerstone was laid for east wing.

1927—March 2: Fire destroyed the temporary "Pasteboard Capitol."

1927—Union soldier statue, the *Soldiers and Sailors Monument*, was erected on Capitol grounds.

1928—January: Construction of east wing finished.

1929—March 2: Legislature approved a special levy to provide revenue for the Capitol Building Fund to fund construction of the main unit of the Capitol.

1930—March 6: The George A. Fuller Company began construction of the Capitol's main unit.

1930—November 5: Cornerstone was laid for the main unit.

1931—Mack, Jenny and Tyler Company gilded the dome for the first time.

1932—June 20: The current Capitol was dedicated.

1934—May 17: Cass Gilbert, architect of the Capitol, died.

1939—Legislature created State Office Building Commission.

1940—Project to improve riverbank in front of Capitol was completed.

1945—July: State Office Building Commission entered into contract with Cass Gilbert Jr. to design Building 3 (long known as the DMV Building).

1946—Third floor was added to Governor's Mansion.

1946—Gold was removed from Capitol dome, which then was painted.

1947—Construction of fountain in Capitol Circle was completed.

1950—Construction of Building 3 finished.

1950—Planning began for Building 4.

1950—West Virginia received replica of Liberty Bell as part of a commemoration of a U.S. Savings Bonds campaign.

1951—Agencies moved into Building 3.

1951—Sound system was installed in House of Delegates chamber.

1952—Construction began on a parking garage on California Avenue that was designed by Cass Gilbert Jr.

1953—Construction was completed on parking garage.

1954—Construction of Building 4 was finished.

1960—Sound system with microphone for each member was installed in Senate chamber.

1968—May 1: Governor Hulett Smith and others broke ground for Buildings 5, 6 and 7 of the Capitol Complex.

1970—Large fountain outside Buildings 5, 6 and 7 was built.

1971—Agriculture Commissioner Gus Douglass had mezzanine built in Capitol's east wing.

1974—June 20: Governor Arch Moore and others dedicated the *Lincoln Walks at Midnight* statue on Capitol grounds.

1976—Capitol Building Commission was reestablished.

1976—July 6: Black-tie affair celebrated completion of the West Virginia Science and Culture Center.

1976—July 11: Culture Center opened to the public.

1976—Administration of Governor Arch Moore awarded contract for Capitol dome to be gilded again.

1977—Governor Jay Rockefeller canceled contract for gilding of dome and bought a snowplow for Preston County with some of the revenue from sale of the gold leaf.

1979—West Virginia Independence Hall, the former U.S. Customs House where plans were made for statehood during the Civil War, became a state museum.

1985—West Virginia Mansion Preservation Foundation was established to raise money for maintenance and furnishings at the Governor's Mansion.

1985—Governor Arch Moore and others dedicated bust of Booker T. Washington on Capitol grounds.

1985—A legislative resolution and an executive order called for building a memorial to veterans of the war in Vietnam, although it eventually became a memorial for veterans of the four major wars of the twentieth century.

1986—January 14: Secretary of State Ken Hechler had stuffed black bear delivered to his office. It became the first of three such bears to be displayed first at his office and then in front of the attorney general's office.

1986—The legislature let the Capitol Building Commission be terminated.

1987—A commission selected Joseph Mullins to design the Veterans Memorial.

1988—Portion of Washington Street that ran through Capitol Complex was closed.

1988—Gilding of Capitol dome began.

1989—August 14: Governor Gaston Caperton dedicated the site of the Veterans Memorial Plaza.

1990—May 19: *Fallen Partner* statue was dedicated on terrace of Culture Center.

1990—June 20: Governor Gaston Caperton and others celebrated the partial completion of the project to gild the Capitol dome, which was finished six months later.

1990—July 1: The Capitol Building Commission was reestablished as a result of new legislation.

1991—Foundation for Veterans Memorial was completed.

1992—Mezzanine in Capitol's east wing was removed.

1992—Murals on ceilings of west and east wings were refurbished.

1994—Legislature allocated a portion of lottery revenues for completion of the Veterans Memorial.

1994—September 9: *Fallen Firefighter Memorial* was dedicated on terrace of Culture Center.

1995—House of Delegates chamber received its most extensive refurbishing since it went into use in 1932.

1995—November 11: The West Virginia Veterans Memorial was dedicated, although its four sculptures were not yet installed.

1996—Inside of Capitol dome was repainted completely for first time since building's dedication.

1996—Plaza on south side of Capitol was expanded following design Cass Gilbert Sr. prepared more than six decades earlier.

1997—January 11: Governor Gaston Caperton, Senator Jay Rockefeller and others dedicated a statue of Senator Robert Byrd, who was present, in the rotunda of the Capitol.

1999—Legislature made first appropriation for extensive renovation of the State Museum.

1999—Legislature approved the commissioning of a statue to honor female veterans.

1999—New parking garage was built at northwestern corner of the campus near Greenbrier and Piedmont Streets.

1999—November 11: Governor Cecil Underwood unveiled the statue of the Vietnam War marine, the last of four sculptures to be installed at the Veterans Memorial.

2001—May: Division of Culture and History bid successfully in auction for Cass Gilbert's original drawings and other documents about the Capitol.

2001—November 9: Bust of Mother's Day founder Anna Jarvis was dedicated on ground floor of Capitol rotunda.

2002—November: Problems with the rotunda chandelier led to fears the chandelier might fall and crash through floor.

2003—March 6: Governor Bob Wise and others dedicated the *West Virginia Coal Miner* statue on Capitol grounds.

2003—Sculptor Joseph Mullins revealed his design for the statue honoring female veterans, which became the subject of controversy.

2003—Wise administration demolished parking garage on California Avenue that was designed by Cass Gilbert Jr.

2003—September: New problems renewed fears that rotunda chandelier might fall and crash through floor.

2004—January: State Museum closed to prepare for renovation.

2004—October: Work to repair and gild the Capitol dome began as the dome was wrapped in a plastic sheath.

2005—West Virginians voted over the Internet and by phone for having the panels around the ornaments on the Capitol dome remain gray while the rest of the dome was gilded.

2005—October: Repairs and gilding of the Capitol dome were completed.

2007—The Executive Mansion Renovation Fund was established as a tax-exempt organization to raise money for work on the Governor's Mansion.

2008—Oklahoma First Lady Kim Henry and West Virginia First Lady Gayle Manchin planted an American elm sapling outside the Capitol. It came from a tree that survived the April 19, 1995 bombing of the federal building in Oklahoma City.

2009—Capitol Building Commission approved the statue of a female veteran designed by Joseph Mullins.

2009—June 20: The newly renovated State Museum opened to the public for the first time in more than five years.

2010—Large fountain outside Buildings 5, 6 and 7 was removed.

2010—December: Building 3 was vacated in preparation for extensive renovations.

2011—Concrete bollards were set up around Capitol grounds and then removed following criticism.

2011—November 11: State officials dedicated statue of female veteran on Capitol grounds.

Bibliography

Charleston Daily Mail, 1921–2012.

Charleston Gazette, 1921–2012.

Cohen, Stan, and Richard Andre. *Capitols of West Virginia: A Pictorial History*. Charleston, WV: Pictorial Histories Publishing Co., 1989.

Craigo, Oshel. Personal interview. June 5, 2012.

Davis, Leonard M. "National Register of Historic Place Inventory—Nomination Form for West Virginia State Capitol, West Virginia Executive Mansion." May 9, 1974.

Ferguson, Rob. Personal interview. June 5, 2012.

Gwinn, Sherman. "These Brothers Take Houses for a Ride!" *American Magazine*, April 1925.

Morgan, John G. *Charleston 175*. Charleston, WV: Charleston Gazette, 1970.

Peyton, Billy Joe. "West Virginia: Birth of a State and the Strange Case of the Floating Capital." Lecture at the Clay Center for the Arts and Sciences of West Virginia, Charleston, WV, March 14, 2012.

Senate of West Virginia. *The West Virginia Capitol: A Commemorative History*. Charleston: Senate of West Virginia, 1982.

Sullivan, Ken, editor. *The West Virginia Encyclopedia*. Charleston: West Virginia Humanities Council, 2006.

About the Author

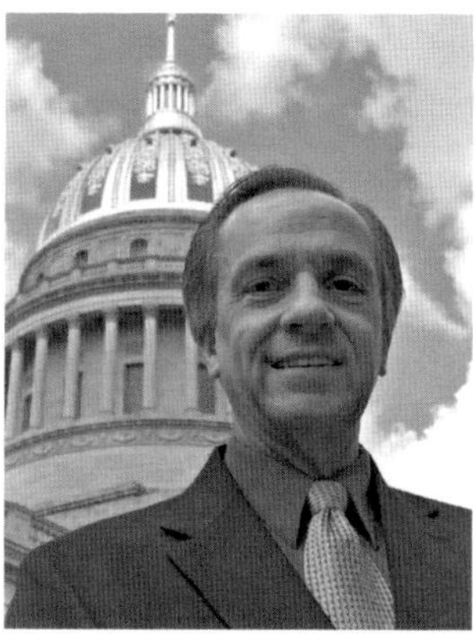

Photo by Rachel Coffman.

Jim Wallace is senior counsel for public relations at TSG Consulting in Charleston. Previously, he was the *Charleston Daily Mail*'s statehouse reporter and news director of West Virginia Public Radio in Charleston. Prior to that, he was news director of WWVA/WOVK radio and then public radio's Northern Panhandle bureau chief in Wheeling. Earlier, he worked for several Ohio radio stations. He has a B.A. from The Ohio State University and an M.S. from West Virginia University. His first book, *The Olmsted Story: A Brief History of Olmsted Falls and Olmsted Township*, published by The History Press, was about his hometown in Ohio.